SUCCESSFUL
JEWELLERY
MAKER

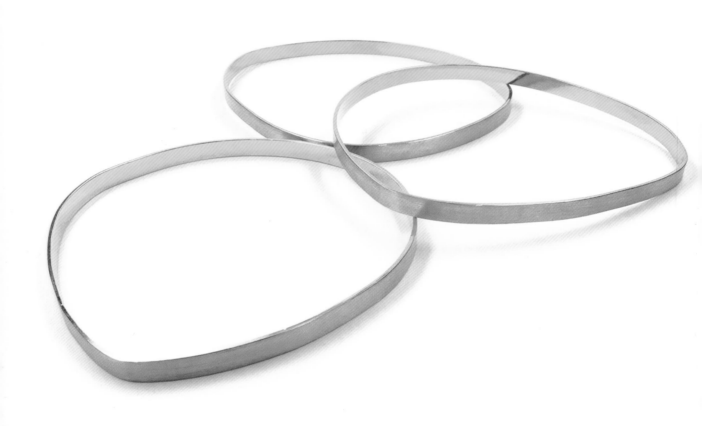

SUCCESSFUL
JEWELLERY
MAKER

Frieda Munro

Search Press

A QUARTO BOOK

Published in 2016 by
Search Press Ltd
Wellwood
North Farm Road
Tunbridge Wells
Kent TN2 3DR

ISBN: 978-1-78221-382-6

Conceived, designed and produced by
Quarto Publishing plc
The Old Brewery
6 Blundell Street
London N7 9BH

QUAR. FIFJ

EDITOR Michelle Pickering
ART DIRECTOR Caroline Guest
DESIGNER Austin Taylor
PHOTOGRAPHER Phil Wilkins
PICTURE RESEARCHER Sarah Bell
INDEXER Diana LeCore
CREATIVE DIRECTOR: Moira Clinch
PUBLISHER: Paul Carslake

Colour separation by Cypress Colours (HK) Ltd, Hong Kong
Printed by 1010 Printing International Ltd China

Contents

1 WHAT'S THE PROBLEM?

2 SHAPING

Foreword

Everyone makes mistakes – it's an inevitable and unavoidable part of the learning process, and often getting it wrong makes us fully grasp how to get it right the next time.

Having said that, getting a process right initially could save you a lot of time and money. This book is intended as a resource for all makers in an attempt to head potential problems off at the pass and to deal with mistakes once they have been made.

It is a good idea to keep a technical journal of your work – note down what works and what doesn't. Catalogue your disasters as well as your triumphs. Jewellery is such a vast subject that you might not use a technique for a couple of years, so having notes to refer back to will be invaluable.

About this book

Beginning with the diagnostic charts in chapter 1, you can see at a glance where the root of your problem lies. Use the following five chapters to find the solution for whatever is preventing you from producing the work you want.

Chapter 1, pages 8–33

The diagnostic charts let you identify a problem, its cause and a solution, either directly from the chart, from the fix-it part of the book or from the best practice articles. Problems are organised by metalwork technique, and flagged to indicate the material affected where appropriate.

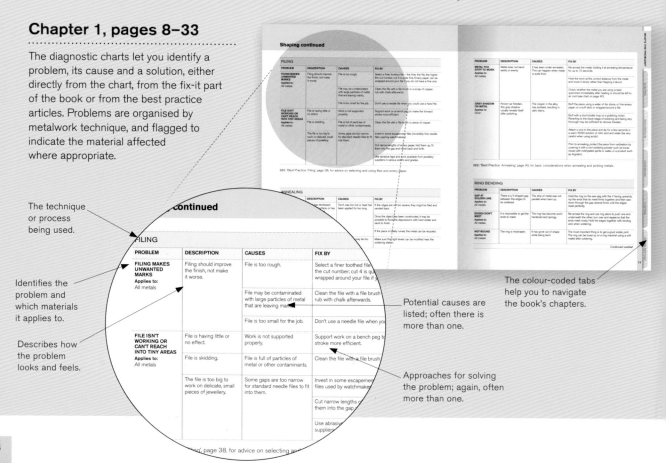

The technique or process being used.

Identifies the problem and which materials it applies to.

Describes how the problem looks and feels.

Potential causes are listed; often there is more than one.

Approaches for solving the problem; again, often more than one.

The colour-coded tabs help you to navigate the book's chapters.

One of the lovely things about making jewellery is that a piece is very rarely a dead loss. Most pieces can be rescued after a mistake and, if worse comes to worst, at least it can be recycled and turned into something else.

Much of the skill in making an object beautifully is down to practice and muscle memory, which can only be achieved by repetition. I remember being in awe of my first teachers, who could saw a straight line with their eyes closed. Being a teacher myself now, I still remember how hard those basic skills first seemed.

Everybody evolves their own ways of working, and hundreds of tricks and techniques will be picked up from others or invented out of necessity. How you end up making your work becomes part of your creative language and your signature style. I hope this book will help to provide a solid foundation upon which great pieces can be made (even if they have to be rescued along the way).

Firda

Chapters 2–6, pages 34–169

These chapters are organised by the metalwork techniques being used. Within each chapter are two types of content: best practice and fix-its. Each chapter is introduced with best practice topics that help to lay the foundations for problem-free techniques. In the fix-it sections, faults are described in detail, causes discussed and solutions offered.

Beautiful finished pieces are featured to demonstrate what can be achieved in each area.

Key stages of the technique are demonstrated.

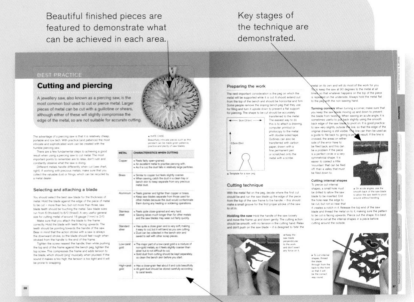

Best practice article ▶
Best practice articles describe the ideal way of working for each stage of the jewellery-making process.

Charts are dotted throughout to provide at-a-glance reference points.

Images of the faults aid easy diagnosis of the problem.

◀ Fix-it article
The fix-it section of each chapter looks at the most common problems jewellery makers come across and describes approaches for troubleshooting.

Specific solutions are suggested when a particular cause is known.

Photographs demonstrate the best ways to remedy the issue at hand.

WHAT'S THE PROBLEM?

The diagnostic charts in this section have been designed as a first point of reference and identify many of the common problems that jewellery makers come up against. The main issue is to recognise where you are going wrong, so several options for possible causes are listed along with suggestions for ways to remedy the problem.

Shaping

CUTTING AND PIERCING

PROBLEM	DESCRIPTION	CAUSES	FIX BY
CAN'T SAW A STRAIGHT LINE Applies to: All metals	The saw will not stay straight.	The saw blade is not tight enough.	Loosen one nut, then push the edge of the saw frame below the nut against the bench peg and retighten the nut.
		The blade has been put on upside down.	The teeth should point towards the handle; when you stroke the blade away from the handle end, it should feel rough.
		The saw peg is not secure.	Cutting on a surface that moves with every stroke is difficult. Tighten the screw that allows the saw peg to pivot.
CAN'T SEE WHAT TO CUT Applies to: All metals	If you cannot see what should be cut, then cutting it will be challenging!	The transcribed design is hard to read on the metal.	The clearest method is to tape a printed or photocopied design on to the metal. If drawing the design on to the metal, use a fine-tipped permanent pen so that the drawing does not get rubbed off before sawing is finished. If scribing a design, try to keep strokes to a minimum.
		A poorly lit working environment.	Supplement natural light with an anglepoise lamp with a bright bulb. This can be tilted to catch the light on a scribed design.
		Your seat is at the wrong height.	Jewellery benches tend to be slightly higher than normal workbenches (90cm/36in), so use an adjustable seat.
SAW BLADE BREAKS Applies to: All metals	Repeated breaking of saw blades is frustrating and slows down progress.	Saw blade is too fine.	Adjust the blade size you are using. There should be between two and three teeth in contact with the metal at any one time.
		Metal has jumped up on the peg, twisting the blade.	Hold the metal firmly down on the saw peg with your non-sawing hand.
		Too much pressure used.	Don't push when sawing – the blade will do the work for you.
		Only a small part of the blade has been used when sawing.	Saw with long strokes using all the teeth.
		Blade has twisted when going around a corner.	Always keep the blade moving up and down when going around corners to prevent it from twisting.
		Blade is under too much tension.	The blade should be taut, but too much tension will cause it to snap.
SAW BLADE GETS STUCK Applies to: All metals	The blade refuses to move up or down.	Blade has been pushed too hard into the material.	Stop trying to move the blade forwards, then try to move it gently up and down. It may be necessary to loosen the top nut and pull the blade out of the piece. Try lubricating the back of the blade with wax or saliva.
		Blade has become twisted.	Release your hold on the metal and allow the blade to return to its natural position before resuming.

SEE: 'Best Practice: Cutting and Piercing', page 36, to learn how to cut or pierce different types of metal accurately.

FILING

PROBLEM	DESCRIPTION	CAUSES	FIX BY
FILING MAKES UNWANTED MARKS Applies to: All metals	Filing should improve the finish, not make it worse.	File is too rough.	Select a finer toothed file – the finer the file, the higher the cut number; cut 4 is quite fine. Emery paper can be wrapped around your file if you do not have a fine one.
		File may be contaminated with large particles of metal that are leaving marks.	Clean the file with a file brush or a scrap of copper; rub with chalk afterwards.
		File is too small for the job.	Don't use a needle file when you could use a hand file.
FILE ISN'T WORKING OR CAN'T REACH INTO TINY AREAS Applies to: All metals	File is having little or no effect.	Work is not supported properly.	Support work on a bench peg to make the forward stroke more efficient.
	File is skidding.	File is full of particles of metal or other contaminants.	Clean the file with a file brush or piece of copper.
	The file is too big to work on delicate, small pieces of jewellery.	Some gaps are too narrow for standard needle files to fit into them.	Invest in some escapement files (incredibly fine needle files used by watchmakers).
			Cut narrow lengths of emery paper, fold them up, fit them into the gap and move back and forth.
			Use abrasive tape and cord, available from jewellery suppliers in various widths and grades.

SEE: 'Best Practice: Filing', page 38, for advice on selecting and using files and emery paper.

ANNEALING

PROBLEM	DESCRIPTION	CAUSES	FIX BY
METAL HAS MELTED Applies to: All metals	Metal has developed ridges on surface, or has totally collapsed.	Torch was too hot or heat has been applied for too long.	If the ridges are not too severe, they might be filed and sanded back.
			Once the object has been constructed, it may be possible to flood the depressions with hard solder and sand to finish.
			If the piece is totally ruined, the metal can be recycled.
		Soldering area may be too brightly lit.	Make sure that light levels can be modified near the soldering station.

PROBLEM	DESCRIPTION	CAUSES	FIX BY
METAL TOO STIFF TO WORK Applies to: All metals	Metal does not bend easily or evenly.	It has been under-annealed. This can happen when metal is quite thick.	Re-anneal the metal, holding it at annealing temperature for up to 10 seconds.
			Hold the torch at the correct distance from the metal and move it slowly rather than flapping it about.
			Check whether the metal you are using is best quenched immediately after heating or should be left to air cool (see chart on page 40).
GREY SHADOW ON METAL Applies to: Silver	Known as firestain, this grey shadow usually reveals itself after polishing.	The copper in the alloy has oxidised, resulting in dark stains.	Buff the piece using a water of Ayr stone, or fine emery paper on a buff stick or wrapped around a file.
			Buff with a short bristle mop on a polishing motor. Reverting to the tripoli stage of polishing and being very thorough may be sufficient to remove firestain.
			Attach a wire to the piece and dip for a few seconds in a warm 50:50 solution of nitric acid and water (be very careful when using acids).
			Prior to annealing, protect the piece from oxidisation by covering it with a non-oxidising powder such as borax mixed with methylated spirits or water, or a product such as Argotect.

SEE: 'Best Practice: Annealing', page 40, for basic considerations when annealing and pickling metals.

RING BENDING

PROBLEM	DESCRIPTION	CAUSES	FIX BY
GAP AT SOLDER LINE Applies to: All metals	There is a V-shaped gap between the edges to be soldered.	The strip of metal was not parallel when bent up.	Hold the ring on the saw peg with the V facing upwards, nip the ends that do meet firmly together and then saw down through the gap several times until the edges meet perfectly.
EDGES DON'T MEET Applies to: All metals	It is impossible to get the ends to meet.	The ring has become work-hardened and springy.	Re-anneal the ring and use ring pliers to push one end underneath the other; turn over and repeat so that the ends meet nicely. Hold the edges together with binding wire when soldering.
NOT ROUND Applies to: All metals	The ring is misshapen.	It has gone out of shape while being bent.	The most important thing is to get a good solder joint. The ring can be trued up on a ring mandrel using a soft mallet after soldering.

Continued overleaf

Shaping continued

PROBLEM	DESCRIPTION	CAUSES	FIX BY
RING IS WRONG SIZE Applies to: All metals	Once soldered together, the ring turns out to be the wrong size.	Fingers change size depending on the temperature and ring stick sizes vary slightly. It could also be simple miscalculation.	To enlarge a ring, anneal it, place it on a mandrel and tap lightly with a hammer. Move the ring around the mandrel to stretch the metal evenly.
			To reduce the size, cut out a small piece on either side of the soldered joint and then re-solder.
			If you have access to a ring sizer, rings can easily be made smaller or larger, although shrinking the size can change the profile.
MARKS ON RING Applies to: All metals	There are ridges along the inside of the shank.	The wrong type of pliers has been used, or ring pliers have been used the wrong way round.	Make sure the curved side of the ring pliers is used on the inside of the ring and the flat face on the outside.
			Anneal the ring and hammer on a mandrel with a soft mallet to remove large ridges. File off the gouges and smooth the metal using emery paper.

SEE: 'Best Practice: Ring Bending', page 42, for advice on achieving the right size ring as well as piercing, shaping and texturing it.

FORGING

PROBLEM	DESCRIPTION	CAUSES	FIX BY
CRACKS IN METAL Applies to: All metals	Split appears in the metal.	It has been under-annealed and the metal has become fatigued.	Saw off the affected part, re-anneal and continue. Minimise stress on the metal by keeping hammer blows in one direction at a time between annealings. Cool the metal in the correct way after annealing (see chart on page 40).
		Annealing at too high a temperature or for too long can cause the metal to become coarse and crack.	If you are near the end of the project, try patching up holes with wire or shims of silver and solder, then file and sand back.
UNWANTED MARKS ON METAL Applies to: All metals	Always stop as soon as you notice any unwanted marks.	There are marks on the face of the hammer.	Stop immediately and file and sand the marks off the piece. Put the hammer in a vice and use abrasive tape (in the same way as when shining shoes) to remove the marks from the hammer face. Polish the hammer face on a polishing motor.
		The face of the hammer is not hitting the work properly, and the hammer edge is making a dent.	This can happen if the piece is positioned too high. Find something stable to stand on.
			Hold the hammer correctly near the end of the handle and bend from the elbow, not the wrist. Adjust your grip so that the face of the hammer hits the work correctly.
		The wrong type of hammer is being used.	Carefully flatten the marks with a planishing hammer.

PROBLEM	DESCRIPTION	CAUSES	FIX BY
METAL IS BENDING Applies to: All metals	When trying to flatten or square up metal, it keeps bending in one direction.	Hammer strokes are weighted on one side.	Concentrate hammer blows on the wider side to try to even up the curve.
		Hammer is not being held properly.	Strike the metal straight on, adjusting the angle at which the hammer is held or the height of the work if necessary.
ROD FRACTURES Applies to: Brass rod	Even with regular annealing, the end of the brass rod keeps fracturing.	Extruded rod is more brittle and prone to cracking than drawn rod.	Saw off the fractured part, re-anneal and continue to work very gently.
			Choose drawn rod.
ROD TURNING INTO TUBE Applies to: All metals	The end of the rod is becoming concave.	As the metal is displaced around the edges, it is moving forwards.	Saw or file off the end whenever this happens and keep hammering. Use a file for the final taper point.
ROD GOING FLAT Applies to: All metals	Rod has lost its squareness.	Rod tends to turn into a rhombus shape, and then can quickly go flat.	Carefully hammer the piece, rotating it regularly and using the hammer strokes to restore the rod to a square shape. If it becomes completely flattened, start again with new rod.

SEE: 'Best Practice: Forging', page 45, for an overview of the various forging tools and guidance on achieving a variety of shapes and forms.

DOMING AND SWAGING

PROBLEM	DESCRIPTION	CAUSES	FIX BY
MARKS ON UNDERSIDE OF DOME Applies to: All metals	What should be a perfect hemisphere has gouges near the edges.	The metal has been forced into too small a hollow on the doming block and the lip has marked the metal.	The disc of metal should fit comfortably into the hollow. Start with a large hollow and work down to the size you want.
			Check that there is no dirt or grit on the hollow before putting the metal into it.
			It may be possible to remove the marks with a file if they are not too deep.
MARKS ON INSIDE OF DOME Applies to: All metals	If the inner face of the dome is on show, this could be a problem.	The punch has marks on it, caused by forcing the punch into too small a hollow, and these marks will transfer to the metal.	Place the punch upright in a vice, use emery paper to sand off the marks and then polish.
			Use emery paper to remove marks from the metal.
UNEVEN INDENTATIONS ON DOME Applies to: All metals	The outer surface of the dome is not smooth.	Using too small a punch on metal does this.	Anneal the dome and use a larger punch. The punch should fit entirely inside the hollow, leaving enough room for the thickness of the metal. As you move down the sizes of hollow, match the punch to the indentation.

Continued overleaf

PROBLEM	DESCRIPTION	CAUSES	FIX BY
SWAGED EDGES DON'T MEET NEATLY **Applies to:** All metals	The edges are not close enough together to solder.	Hammer blows on the edge of the metal have stretched it in parts.	Anneal and then hammer on a metal rod until the edges touch. Run a saw blade down the seam to remove any protruding parts.
HARD TO SWAGE THICK BUT NARROW TUBE **Applies to:** Metal tube	Tube of this kind is often used when making brooch fastenings.	It is hard to bend up narrow lengths of metal greater than 24 gauge (0.5mm).	Swage a wider piece of metal of the correct thickness to form a tube. Add a V shape at the end and use this to pull it through a draw plate until it is the correct diameter, annealing regularly.

SEE: 'Best Practice: Doming and Swaging', page 48, for guidelines on creating perfect domes and tubes.

REPOUSSAGE AND CHASING

PROBLEM	DESCRIPTION	CAUSES	FIX BY
SPLIT ON REPOUSSÉD PIECE **Applies to:** All metals	Always stop as soon as you notice a split appear.	The punch or chasing tool has rough or sharp edges. Metal is too thin or has been under-annealed for the amount it has been stretched.	Remove the piece from the pitch and clean it. Working from the back, fill any gaps with a shim of metal and solder in place with hard solder. File and emery the repair. Be cautious with any further annealing or repoussage work. If there are any sharp areas on the punch or chasing tool, use emery paper to remove them and then repolish the tool.
BUBBLY PITCH **Applies to:** Pitch	Bubbles and/or cracks in the pitch.	It has been overheated.	Gently heat the pitch and use scrap metal to skim off the top bubbly layer. Use minimal heat on the pitch in future.
FORM HAS COLLAPSED **Applies to:** All metals	After being turned, the shape has collapsed.	The metal was not properly supported by the pitch, or the pitch had a bubble in it.	Remove the piece from the pitch and clean it. Replace in the pitch the opposite way up and punch out the collapsed area. Remove, clean and anneal. Pour pitch into the recessed area until flush with the metal. Allow to cool, then replace in the pitch and continue to work.
TOOL SKIDS ON METAL **Applies to:** All metals	The chasing tool or punch keeps slipping.	The hammer might be too heavy in relation to the punch being used.	Select a lighter hammer. If you don't have one, look around for a broad, flat piece of hardwood or a piece of steel to use in place of a hammer.

SEE: 'Best Practice: Repoussage and Chasing', page 50, for basic considerations when choosing and using punches and hammers to create three-dimensional shapes.

SOLDERING

PROBLEM	DESCRIPTION	CAUSES	FIX BY
JOINT HASN'T SOLDERED **Applies to:** All metals	Piece has not soldered at all.	The torch flame can cause a draft that blows the pallions of solder away. It can be hard to spot this when the flux bubbles up.	Pickle, rinse and re-solder, paying close attention when you introduce the torch to the piece.
	Pallions are still visible on the piece.	Not enough heat has been applied to allow the solder to run.	Pickle, rinse, reflux and try again. Warm up the whole area around the joint quickly by using a large bushy flame.
		The heat was insufficient but left on the piece so long that the flux has burned away.	
	Solder has balled up rather than running along the joint.	Too much heat was applied to the joint rather than the whole piece, or sufficient heat did not reach the joint.	Remove the balls of solder, pickle and rinse the piece, reflux and solder again.
		Flux has become exhausted or insufficient flux was applied.	
		Dirt or grease has prevented the solder from running.	
SOLDER HAS RUN BUT JOINT UNSUCCESSFUL **Applies to:** All metals	There is a gap in the seam after soldering.	The joint does not fit together perfectly – solder won't bridge a gap.	Saw open the section that has joined. Run a saw blade through the gap until the joint is light-tight. The blade acts as a tiny file, taking a small piece off each side of the joint.
		The piece or your hands are not thoroughly clean – solder will not flow over contaminants.	Make sure that the piece and your hands are scrupulously clean and free from grease.
	Solder has melted but remains on one side of joint, rather than bridging it.	The heat was concentrated on one side of the joint.	Pickle, rinse, reflux and apply heat more on the opposite side. Try to use the heat of the torch to pull the solder around to where you need it.
		Edges of the joint are not a perfect fit.	Run a saw blade down through the gap, repeating several times as necessary to get a good, tight fit.
	Joint has broken. This sometimes happens once you put a ring on the mandrel to true it up.	This might be due to not enough solder or too widely spread flux.	Run a sheet of emery down the joint to remove contaminants, then scrub with liquid detergent. Use a fine paintbrush to apply flux precisely where it is needed, then re-solder, using binding wire to hold the edges of the joint together if necessary. When soldering a ring, start the heat at the opposite end from the solder seam. This will cause the metal to expand slightly, pushing the joint closer together.
		Overheating can cause the solder to be absorbed into the metal.	
		Contaminants on the seam.	

Continued overleaf

PROBLEM	DESCRIPTION	CAUSES	FIX BY
METAL HAS MOVED WHILE BEING SOLDERED Applies to: All metals	Pieces being joined no longer meet as they should.	Metal can stretch and move slightly when heated, resulting in its position changing during the soldering process.	Use heat to separate the elements that have joined badly, pickle and clean them, then re-solder. Any tension in the metal should have been removed by heating.
			For future projects, try annealing elements before setting them up for soldering. This should get any movement out of the way in advance.
BUBBLES AND PITS ON JOINT Applies to: All metals	Seam is visible because of bubbling.	In its liquid state solder can react with atmospheric gases, which can become trapped as tiny bubbles when the solder solidifies. This can happen if the metal or the solder is dirty, or if too much heat has been applied. It can also be the result of repeated solderings that have caused the alloys to decompose slightly. It is most obvious when an excessive amount of solder has been used.	Pickle and rinse the piece, then file off excess solder. Reflux, bind with binding wire if necessary and heat until the solder flows again. You may need to add some more solder.
CHAIN LINKS SOLDERED TOGETHER Applies to: All metals	Chain becomes stiff and does not hang properly.	Solder has run on to the wrong part of the chain, fusing two links together.	Hold one of the fused links in tweezers in a third hand. Play a flame over both fused links and use another pair of tweezers to gently wiggle them apart. Keep moving the link after removing the flame until you are sure it will not re-solder.
JUMP RINGS FALL OFF Applies to: All metals	Although solder has run, jump rings are not strongly attached.	There is not enough metal making contact for a stable joint.	File a flat area where the jump ring attaches to the main piece. This creates a more stable contact area and will not be noticeable once the piece is finished.
		The jump ring did not get hot enough because the reverse-action tweezers acted as a heat sink.	Use fine stainless steel tweezers to hold the jump ring – these will allow more heat to reach it.
EAR POSTS OR PIN BACKS MELT Applies to: All metals	Posts and pins melt in the heat.	When attaching small or thin pieces of metal to a larger piece, the latter will require much more heat to get up to temperature than the tiny pieces.	Heat the melted post until the solder runs, then pick it off. Pickle and rinse. When re-soldering, watch the solder very carefully and remove the heat as soon as it runs.
			Note that there is usually no need to heat ear posts or other small pieces when soldering them on to something large because they will pick up sufficient heat from the main piece and the hearth.

SEE: 'Best Practice: Soldering', page 52, for a detailed review of soldering tools, materials and methods, plus additional techniques for joining metals.

RIVETING

PROBLEM	DESCRIPTION	CAUSES	FIX BY
RIVET HAS FAILED **Applies to:** All metals	Both parts of the piece have separated.	Ends of the rivet are not folded back enough to grip the pieces of metal together. The rivet may have been too short or filed down too much, or the hole might be too big.	Remove the rivet by hammering it out over an indentation in a doming block, or by using a centre punch or scribe to push the rivet out. Remake the rivet, taking care that a small amount protrudes from top and bottom so that it can be hammered back sufficiently.
RIVET HAS BENT **Applies to:** All metals	Bent rivet.	Rivet was too long.	Remove the rivet. If this is difficult to do, file the rivet right back and use a centre punch over a doming block or open vice to tap it out. Then make a shorter rivet.
RIVET NOT ACTING AS A PIVOT **Applies to:** All metals	Tight rivet that stops other elements of the piece from moving.	There should have been a small space left between the metal being joined and the rivet in order to allow movement.	Work the rivet back and forth to try to loosen it. Use some liquid detergent as a lubricant to help achieve this. If you cannot loosen the rivet, remove it by drilling through it and then make a new one. Insert a piece of thick paper between the elements being joined to create a gap while you fit the rivet. Then burn away the paper or, if the piece cannot be heated, soak it in water and pull the paper free.
RIVET WORKS LOOSE **Applies to:** All metals	Loose rivet.	The rivet head is too small for the flexibility of the material.	Make some washers to give the rivet a solid base for attachment and to prevent the rivet from working free. Washers can be a decorative element, or they can be purely functional and as simple as a small circle with a hole.

SEE: 'Best Practice: Riveting', page 58, for advice on making a variety of rivets, from countersunk to tube rivets.

Shaping continued

HINGES

PROBLEM	DESCRIPTION	CAUSES	FIX BY
HINGE FROZEN TOGETHER Applies to: All metals	Excess solder has flowed between the knuckles of the hinge.	Too much solder or insufficient antiflux has been used.	Run a very fine (8/0) saw blade down the hinges to loosen them.
			If that does not work, reheat until the solder runs and separate the pieces. It would be safest to make new knuckles. Carefully antiflux the side where you do not want the solder to flow, then re-solder.
PIECE SOLDERED TOGETHER Applies to: All metals	The part that should open is soldered shut.	Excess heat or inadequate antiflux has caused the solder to run where it is not wanted.	Try separating the pieces using a fine saw blade (8/0) or by hammering a utility knife blade between them.
			If that fails, reheat until the solder flows again and take apart. Use emery paper to remove any solder that might cause this to happen again, then re-solder.
HINGE LOOSE Applies to: All metals	Loose hinge.	Hinge pin is too thin.	Make a new hinge pin using thicker wire. Lubricate it with some wax and then twist it into the hinge knuckles for a tight fit.
HINGE PIN WON'T FIT Applies to: All metals	Despite twisting and lubricating, hinge pin will not fit into knuckles.	Knuckles have moved during soldering and no longer align.	Try opening and moving the pieces to see if the pin will slide in. If it won't, check to see which part is misaligned. Protect all other joints from heat and reposition the affected knuckle, protecting the other parts of the hinge with plenty of antiflux.
		A burr of metal is stuck in the tube.	Check that there is nothing inside the tube preventing the hinge pin from getting through. If there is, carefully drill it out using a drill bit held in a pin vice.
		Hinge pin is too wide.	Hold the pin in a pin vice and file it down while turning it. Keep checking until it fits tightly into the hinge.
PIECE NO LONGER ALIGNS PROPERLY Applies to: All metals	Sometimes when a hinged object is closed, the back and front do not align perfectly.	One half may have slipped slightly when being constructed.	Put the piece on end and lightly hammer the part that protrudes until it aligns once more. File and sand off any hammer marks this causes. If the misalignment is too obvious, start again.
		The bearing for the hinge was not properly filed.	
PIECE NO LONGER CLOSES PERFECTLY Applies to: All metals	There are gaps around the lip of the object.	The metal has deformed slightly when being heated.	Note where the piece closes tightly, then insert a fine piece of steel, such as a utility knife blade, in that part. Close the piece and exert some pressure on it. Continue doing this all around until it closes nicely.

SEE: 'Best Practice: Hinges', page 60, for an overview of common hinges used in jewellery.

Decoration

ROLLING MILL

PROBLEM	DESCRIPTION	CAUSES	FIX BY
MARKS ON THE WORK Applies to: All metals	Mystery marks have appeared on the work.	The rollers have dirt or other debris on them.	Remove any dirt and debris and wipe the rollers clean with wire wool.
		The rollers have been permanently damaged.	Avoid the area if it is small.
			Send the rollers to be re-machined.
TEXTURE NOT CLEAR Applies to: All metals	Hardly any impression has been made on the metal.	The metal is not properly annealed.	Re-anneal the metal and roll again.
		The rollers are not tight enough.	Try again with the rollers slightly tighter.
		The texturing material is not robust enough.	Choose a different texturing material that is not too soft.
METAL IS STUCK Applies to: All metals	The handle will not turn forwards.	The rollers are too close together and are trying to displace more metal than they can cope with.	Reverse the metal out of the rollers, widen the gap between them and try again.
METAL HAS DEFORMED Applies to: All metals	A square piece of metal comes out a rhombus.	The metal was not inserted perpendicular to the rollers.	Trim the metal into a square shape again.
			Start with a fresh square of metal.
	The metal is bent into a banana-shaped curve.	It was not fed into the rollers perpendicular.	Hold the metal perpendicular to your workbench with the curved edge upwards and use a soft mallet to hammer it straight again.
		The rollers are not set evenly.	Move the rollers until they are almost touching and check that the gap between them is even on each side. Adjust if necessary (refer to your machine's user manual to do this).
	Metal is bumpy.	Metal is under-annealed.	Re-anneal and roll again a few times before tightening the rollers any further.
		Metal has been put under too much pressure too quickly.	Tighten the rollers by a quarter turn at a time, not by a massive increment.
CRACKED EDGE Applies to: All metals	When milling down a thick piece of metal, a crack has appeared.	Metal is under-annealed.	Cut off the cracked piece and anneal again before re-rolling.

SEE: 'Best Practice: Rolling Mill', page 86, for guidance on how to mill down metal and add texture to it.

Decoration continued

HAMMERS AND PUNCHES

PROBLEM	DESCRIPTION	CAUSES	FIX BY
HOMEMADE PUNCH UNSATISFACTORY **Applies to:** Tool steel	The texture is not the effect you want.	The punch does not meet your requirements.	Reheat the punch, then reshape the end of it and re-temper.
	Pattern is flaking off the punch.	The punch was under-tempered.	Fix as described above.
PUNCH MARK UNEVEN **Applies to:** All punches	Depression is uneven.	The punch has not been held or hammered at 90 degrees to the metal.	If the impression is light, flatten the metal using a planishing hammer or by sanding back, then re-anneal and try again.
HAMMERED METAL TOO THIN **Applies to:** All metals	Metal becomes very thin and may be warped.	The amount of hammer blows is too great for the thickness of metal.	Save the metal for another project and start again, making some test pieces first to judge how thick the initial metal needs to be.
RING TOO LARGE BUT TEXTURING NOT FINISHED **Applies to:** All metals	Ring is only half textured and is already the right size or too large.	Underestimating how far the ring will stretch in relation to the texture required.	Saw out a couple of millimetres at the solder seam (allowing for more hammering as required). Re-solder the seam, pickle and continue with texturing.
SPELLING MISTAKE OR LETTER UPSIDE DOWN **Applies to:** All metals	The lettering is incorrect.	Human error – accidents do happen.	File and emery the mistake away and then re-punch the lettering.
			If the mistake is on silver, flood it with solder at the end of the job and re-punch the text.

SEE: 'Best Practice: Hammers and Punches', page 88, for advice on using hammers and punches to texture metal.

ETCHING

PROBLEM	DESCRIPTION	CAUSES	FIX BY
BLURRY EDGES ON ETCHING **Applies to:** All metals	Not a crisp outline.	The acid solution is too strong and has undercut the resist.	Start again, diluting the solution further and allowing longer for the metal to etch.
		The resist did not dry properly or was too thin at the edges.	Start again.
PNP IMAGE DOES NOT TRANSFER PROPERLY **Applies to:** All metals	Black image comes off on the film.	The ink did not get hot enough to release properly.	Heat the metal on a hotplate or the surface of the iron for a few minutes before applying the transfer and keep ironing until the black image shows clearly through the blue paper.
PNP IMAGE HAS GONE BLACK **Applies to:** All metals	No detail has transferred to the metal.	It has been ironed for too long and the image has melted.	Clean off the black image with white spirit and iron on a new one.

PROBLEM	DESCRIPTION	CAUSES	FIX BY
RESIST FLAKES OFF IN ACID **Applies to:** All metals	Fragments of resist are visible in the acid.	Metal not properly degreased.	Remove from the acid as soon as you notice the resist coming off. Rinse well, dry and reapply resist as necessary.
		PnP not adequately heated to bond to metal.	
		Acid might be too strong.	Dilute the acid.
IMAGE IS REVERSED **Applies to:** All metals	Black areas appear white and vice versa.	You have not reversed the original image or design. Remember that anything not protected from the acid will appear darker.	Use an image-editing package such as Photoshop to make a photo negative.
			Reverse the image by copying it on to acetate and then place this with the image facing up in the photocopier.
FRESH ACID WORKING SLOWLY **Applies to:** Nitric acid	Although the same concentration as previous batch, it is very slow.	Acid solutions tend to be less active to start with, then become more active before eventually tailing off again.	Keep a small amount of the old solution to kick-start the new batch.

SEE: 'Best Practice: Etching', page 90, for application methods for using nitric acid and resists to etch metal.

RETICULATION

PROBLEM	DESCRIPTION	CAUSES	FIX BY
DIFFICULTY GETTING DESIRED EFFECT **Applies to:** Silver and brass	The end result does not meet requirements.	It is an unpredictable process by nature, but drafts of air can affect it.	Use different torches to get greater temperature control. Build firebricks around the piece to minimise drafts.
	Patchy or uniform grey tone on silver.	The successive heatings of reticulation often result in firestain.	Cover firestain with silver or gold plating.
			Bright dip the piece in a 50:50 solution of nitric acid and warm water.
METAL HAS SHRUNK OR HOLE HAS APPEARED **Applies to:** Silver and brass	The edges pull in during reticulation.	When metal melts, it pools towards the centre and the edges shrink inwards.	Try again using a thicker gauge of metal to allow for shrinkage.
	Sometimes one or two holes can appear.	Too much heat has been applied to one area and it has melted through.	Redesign the piece to incorporate the hole as a negative space or for setting a stone.
BUCKLED ON UNDERSIDE **Applies to:** Silver and brass	It looks fine on the top, but the underneath has also reticulated.	The metal has been pushed into dramatic ridges, causing the reverse to become bumpy.	Set the reticulated piece in a bezel (as for stone setting) to give it a smooth underside.
			If using it for a ring, add a smooth lining and flare back the ends on a couple of doming punches.

SEE: 'Best Practice: Reticulation', page 93, for how to reticulate metal for decorative effect.

Decoration continued

PLATING

PROBLEM	DESCRIPTION	CAUSES	FIX BY
UNWANTED MATT FINISH **Applies to:** All metals	A matt finish remains matt after plating.	The finish may have been overlooked, or you might have changed your mind.	Barrel polishing briefly might brighten it up a little.
			Polish it and then replate.
PLATING IS PATCHY **Applies to:** All metals	There are 'watermarks' on the work.	This may have occurred when the work was being dried after plating.	Rub with a silver cloth or scrub gently with liquid detergent. Barrel polish it briefly.
			Return it to the plating company.
COLOUR DIFFERS FROM LAST BATCH **Applies to:** All metals	Two pieces don't match.	Concentrations of chemicals in plating bath vary slightly over time.	Take both pieces back to plating company and they will replate one or both of them to match.
PLATING NO LONGER WANTED **Applies to:** All metals	The plating does not produce the look you are after.	You might decide that the plated colour does not work with the piece.	Remove small areas of plate using abrasive means such as emery. To remove all the plate, find a company who can strip the piece chemically.

SEE: 'Best Practice: Plating', page 94, for advice on preparing your work for plating.

PATINATION

PROBLEM	DESCRIPTION	CAUSES	FIX BY
PATINA IS UNSATISFACTORY **Applies to:** All patinas	Scaly and brittle.	Too much patina has built up too quickly or the piece has been exposed to the chemicals repeatedly.	Scrub off with a stiff brush or soap and pumice, or heat up and pickle. Reapply patina, rinsing between coats, and rub with a soft brush. If the problem persists, dilute the oxidising solution.
	Patchy, uneven surface quality.	The piece is not grease-free.	Remove patina as above, taking care not to touch the piece with your fingers, then reapply.
		Solution applied unevenly.	Dip the piece briefly in the solution.
	Cupric nitrate has turned black.	It has been overheated.	Quench the piece and reapply the patina, taking care not to overheat it.
	Silver may have been preferable after all…	You might decide that another colour would be better.	Heat the piece up with a torch, quench and pickle, then apply a different patina if required.
PATINA IS FLAKING OFF **Applies to:** All patinas	The colour is good, but it will not stick.	The surface of the piece is too shiny and the patina cannot adhere.	Abrade the surface with fairly fine emery paper (800–1000 grit) to provide enough texture for the solution to stick to.

SEE: 'Best Practice: Patination', page 95, for guidelines on adding decorative patinas to metal.

POLISHING

PROBLEM	DESCRIPTION	CAUSES	FIX BY
DETAIL MISSING FROM PIECE Applies to: All metals	After completing the polishing process, some fine detail has vanished.	The piece has been pushed too firmly on to the polishing mop and the detail has worn away.	Retexture the piece, then repolish it carefully.
		Too much time was spent on the first stage of polishing.	
NOT SHINY ENOUGH Applies to: All metals	Despite spending some time on the mop, the piece of jewellery is not highly polished.	Too much polishing compound has been applied to the piece and the mop has slipped over it.	Clean the piece of jewellery with liquid detergent, hot water and a toothbrush and repolish using less compound.
		Mop has been contaminated with a coarser polishing compound.	Hold a wire brush against the mop to clean it, or launder the mop in a washing machine.
SCRATCHES OR A DARK SHADOW HAVE APPEARED Applies to: All metals	After final polishing, scratches are visible.	Rouge often reveals the fact that the piece was not properly finished at an earlier stage.	Depending on how deep the scratches look, either revert to the tripoli (coarse polish) stage or re-emery the piece.
			Flood deep scratches or valleys with solder and re-abrade.
	A dark shadow has appeared on silver.	Firestain is caused when the copper in the silver alloy oxidises as a result of being heated. It is often only revealed when the final polishing is done.	Remove firestain by emerying the piece, rubbing it with a water of Ayr stone or using a short bristle brush on the polishing motor.
			Silver plating will cover the problem without damaging any texture.
PIECE HAS BEEN THROWN OFF THE MOP Applies to: All metals	When polishing, the piece can sometimes be grabbed by the mop.	A thread from the mop may have caught on the piece of work. Sometimes grip is lost because the polishing compound is hot and slippery.	If the work is being polished on a polishing motor, it should be easy to find as it usually falls behind the mop. The work may be scratched, though.
			If using a micromotor or pendant drill, it may have flown quite far. Try to calculate the trajectory. The foot of a pair of tights put over the end of a vacuum cleaner can be very useful in recovering lost treasure.

SEE: 'Best Practice: Polishing', page 100, for an overview of how to achieve the best polished finish.

Wirework

PREPARING THE WIRE

PROBLEM	DESCRIPTION	CAUSES	FIX BY
WIRE NOT MOVING SMOOTHLY **Applies to:** All metals	Wire is jerking through the draw plate.	Wire needs to be re-annealed.	Re-anneal the wire.
		Wire not sufficiently lubricated.	Apply light machine oil or beeswax to the wire.
DRAW BENCH TOO SHORT **Applies to:** All metals	Wire required is longer than draw bench.	Most draw benches are about 1.8m (6ft) long.	Pull the wire through the draw plate manually. If the wire is very thin, use parallel pliers to pull it through.
			Reset the tongs near the draw plate and carry on pulling the wire through (this may mark the wire).
TONGS SLIPPING **Applies to:** All metals	Unable to get the tongs to grip the wire.	The point in the wire is not long enough to grip.	Extend the length of the point with a file until it can be easily gripped by the tongs.
		Oil or lubricant has been deposited on the wire or the tongs.	Clean the tongs and the tip of the wire with degreaser.

SEE: 'Best Practice: Preparing the Wire', page 114, for how to anneal, reshape, resize and straighten wire.

MAKING JUMP RINGS

PROBLEM	DESCRIPTION	CAUSES	FIX BY
RING ISN'T ROUND **Applies to:** All metals	Jump ring looks asymmetrical or is not sitting flat.	Wire has not been wrapped around former tightly enough or has not been packed together neatly.	Always wrap the wire tightly around the former and regularly tap it down on the former to keep the spring neat and tight.
		Rings have not been cut straight.	Hold small spirals of rings in parallel pliers to keep them still when sawing.
		Wire has not been sufficiently annealed.	Anneal the jump ring and reform it on round-nose pliers or a suitable former, and tap flat with a soft mallet.
WRONG SIZE **Applies to:** All metals	A jump ring can be too tight to allow movement or too loose for a chain weave to work.	The former was not the right size.	Check the size of the former with a vernier. If using round-nose pliers or a tapered triblet, mark the correct part to wrap wire around with a permanent pen.
		Wire was not properly annealed.	Re-anneal wire and remake jump ring.
HARD TO SAW COIL OF WIRE **Applies to:** All metals	The saw is mangling the jump rings; it is hard to get started.	The wire can jerk about when the saw tries to bite into the metal.	Hold small coils in parallel pliers to keep them still when sawing. For larger coils, use a wooden dowel as a former that can be sawn into, or modify the bench peg to create a protrusion on which the spring can rest for sawing. Try wrapping masking tape around the coil.
		Wire is work-hardened and therefore springy.	

SEE: 'Best Practice: Making Jump Rings', page 116, for how to make jump rings in different sizes and in batches.

CHAIN MAKING

PROBLEM	DESCRIPTION	CAUSES	FIX BY
SOLDER BLOWS OFF JUMP RINGS Applies to: All metals	Not all jump rings on the soldering board are being soldered.	The draft caused by the torch is blowing the pallions off.	Drop the soldier pallions into the flux when cutting them to give them a good coating and help make them stick. Try resting the open end of the jump ring on top of the fluxed solder, or use a soldering pick to apply the solder.
METAL MELTS Applies to: Fine silver	The ends are separating rather than fusing.	Too much heat has been applied.	Don't put jump rings too close together on the soldering board. Move the torch immediately after seeing a 'flash' on the joint, which indicates that the metal has melted.
SOLDER FLOWS TO WRONG PART OF CHAIN Applies to: All metals	Chain is becoming fused together.	Solder will run to the hottest area or to where the flux is.	Use a fine flux brush and a small amount of solder. Only expose the link you are soldering above the reverse-action tweezers, so that you can use the tweezers as a heat sink.
			Apply heat to the fused part while keeping it moving. Remove the heat and continue moving the links until the metal cools.
CHAIN NOT BEHAVING AS IT SHOULD Applies to: All metals	Chain is thick or too spindly.	The ratio of wire thickness to inside diameter is wrong.	Make a test piece to check that the ratio is correct. Keep detailed notes for future chain projects. Remake jump rings to a better ratio or choose another method to fit the ones you have.
MISTAKE OR LOST PLACE IN THE WEAVE Applies to: Complex chain weaves	Chain does not look right.	Often mistakes are made early in the chain when the rhythm is being learned.	Continue until the chain is the right length, mark the first correct link after the mistake and dismantle the chain from the beginning up to this link. Use the jump rings you have removed to carry on the chain. If you notice an error just after it has been made, unpick the chain to before the error and remake.
	Can't remember what to do with the next jump ring.	Picking up the work after a break can lead to confusion.	Carefully compare the chain with the instructions, and try turning it 90 degrees – seeing it from another angle can help. Unpick a couple of links to remind yourself of the rhythm of the chain. If you need to take a break, wrap a piece of wire around the next link to be joined.
CHAIN IS UNEVEN Applies to: All chains	Chain looks unfinished/amateurish.	The chain needs to be trued up.	Push each link on to a knitting needle or scribe held upright in a vice. Attach a wire to the chain and pull it several times through a draw plate or a hole drilled in a piece of wood (see page 119).
LINK HAS SNAPPED Applies to: Fine silver Etruscan chains	A fine silver link has snapped when making Etruscan chain.	Sometimes fused links fail due to insufficient heating or overheating.	Use any suspect links first – they are easy to remove from the end of the chain. As soon as you become aware of a broken link, go back and remove it from the weave. Sometimes you can hear them break, so listen for them.
CHAIN TANGLED IN BARREL POLISHER Applies to: All chains	Lovely finished chain has become a mangled knot.	Long pieces of chain or multiple chains can become very knotted in the barrel polisher.	Lay the chain flat on the bench and gently tease it apart. For fine chain, use two scribes, pins or pieces of wire to do this.
			Prevent tangling by wrapping the whole length of chain in a piece of wire before putting in the barrel.

SEE: 'Best Practice: Chain Making', page 118, for how to make some of the many different types of chains.

Wirework continued

KNITTING AND CROCHET

PROBLEM	DESCRIPTION	CAUSES	FIX BY
WIRE HAS SNAPPED Applies to: All metals	Snapped wire.	The tension is too tight, or the wire has been pulled too tightly.	Loosen the tension on the stitches and unpick a few to leave a tail. Introduce a new length of wire, leaving a long tail that can be woven in and trimmed later.
WIRE IS KINKED Applies to: All metals	Wire has bent back on itself.	A loop of the wire has pulled into an angled kink.	Flatten the kink in flat-nose pliers. If necessary, run a burnisher down it to straighten.
DROPPED STITCHES Applies to: All metals	Stitch has fallen of the needle or the prong on the French knitting dolly.	Sometimes you don't notice a stitch falling off right away.	Stop as soon as you notice and carefully unpick the work until all the stitches are restored.

SEE: 'Best Practice: Knitting and Crochet', page 122, for a brief outline of how to work wire using these needlecraft techniques.

TWISTING WIRE

PROBLEM	DESCRIPTION	CAUSES	FIX BY
WIRES UNRAVEL Applies to: All metals	Wires untwist on being released.	The wire has been under-annealed.	Untwist the wires, form into a neat coil and anneal.
WIRE HAS KNOT IN IT OR HAS SNAPPED Applies to: All metals	A large knot has appeared in the middle of the wire.	The wire has been overtwisted or has not been held taut enough when being wound.	Hold the wire taut and unwind it until the knot untangles, then maintaining the tension, retwist a little.
	Wire has snapped.	Wire has been under-annealed, unevenly annealed or has become weak from being over-annealed.	Wire usually breaks near the end when it has reached its maximum twist.
			If it breaks in the middle, finish twisting the first half, then re-anneal the broken off section and twist that.
NO CHANGE IN APPEARANCE Applies to: All metals	The profile of the wire is the same.	Only wire with angled edges will show the twist.	If you are twisting round wire, it must be twisted on itself. Fold it in half and twist.

SEE: 'Best Practice: Twisting Wire', page 123, for advice on twisting wire for decorative effects.

MAKING SIMPLE FINDINGS

PROBLEM	DESCRIPTION	CAUSES	FIX BY
WIRE LOOKS WOBBLY Applies to: All metals	The lines of the clasp or ear hooks are not flowing smoothly.	The wire needs to be annealed, or the wrong type of pliers has been used.	Anneal the piece and smooth out any bumps with half-round or round-nose pliers.
S CLASP IS WRONGLY MADE OR FAILS Applies to: All metals	Spiral is on wrong side of the S bend.	It is very easy to bend the wire in the wrong direction.	Clasp the whole small spiral so that it is enclosed by a pair of parallel pliers and turn it 180 degrees.
	Can't get the clasp to fasten.	The small spiral is too large to fit through the jump ring on the opposite side.	Compress the small spiral until if fits through.
			Attach a larger loop for the S clasp to fit through.
	The clasp is pulling apart when in use.	The wire used may be too fine.	Remake in thicker gauge wire. The clasp will be stronger if soldered on to the piece. Barrel polish or rub with a burnisher to work-harden it.
		The bracelet may be too tight.	Add a couple of links or an extra jump ring to the bracelet.
EARRING POST WILL NOT GO THROUGH BUTTERFLY Applies to: All metals	Impossible to force the post on.	Commercially made butterflies can be a little tight.	Put both thumbnails between the scrolls to open them up slightly.
			Open up the hole slightly by twisting a broacher or 0.9mm drill bit through it.
TOGGLE CLASP FAILS Applies to: All metals	Toggle won't fit through the loop.	The legs of the T bar may be too long.	Attach the clasp to the jewellery before altering it – it behaves differently on the piece compared to just being held. If the T bar is too long, reduce it gradually, checking it for fit regularly.
		The jump ring on top of the T may be too large or the ring it fits into may be too small.	Re-solder a smaller jump ring on the bar, or make a larger jump ring for the other side.
	Bracelet keeps falling off.	The bracelet is slightly too large, which allows the clasp to unfasten.	Reduce the size of the bracelet.
			Add a safety chain running from either side of the clasp.
EARRINGS DON'T DANGLE PROPERLY Applies to: All metals	Earring hangs at wrong angle or does not move enough.	The weight of the earring is affecting how it hangs on the ear.	Make the hoop either tighter or larger as required on a suitable mandrel or former.
			To increase the movement of the earring, add two small jump rings.

SEE: 'Best Practice: Making Simple Findings', page 124, for guidance on finishing jewellery with your own custom findings.

Casting

CASTING TECHNIQUES

PROBLEM	DESCRIPTION	CAUSES	FIX BY
POOR FINISH ON WAX CARVING **Applies to:** Carving wax	It is very hard to get into some areas.	Fiddly areas in the carving.	It is easier to perfect the finish at the wax-making stage than after casting, so persevere. Try using any little tools you have handy. You can also use small rubber burrs on a micromotor or pendant drill.
WAX HAS SNAPPED OR MISTAKE MADE **Applies to:** Carving wax	A section has broken off the wax.	Wax is quite brittle and it is easy to accidentally knock a bit off.	Use a hot soldering probe or pick to melt the two areas back together. Melt more wax over the break and file back. Allow the wax to recrystallise properly.
	Too much wax has been removed.	More wax has been carved off than was intended.	Melt the surface of the piece with a hot probe or pick, drip some melted wax on it and build up the area in this way.
WAX IS STRINGY **Applies to:** Carving wax	Mozzarella-like strands are being created.	The tool is not hot enough, so the wax is solidifying.	Heat the tool up more, but if wax starts smoking it is too hot.
PLASTER ON CAST **Applies to:** All metals, especially brass and gilding metal	Sometimes investment plaster remains lodged in recesses.	The plaster has bonded to the metal when being cast, and the pickle has not removed it all.	Put it in a strong hot pickle solution for an hour, then clean with a wire brush. Use a small burr to remove the plaster from small recesses. Alternatively, put the piece into an ultrasonic cleaner and scrub with a brass brush.
POROSITY HOLES IN CASTING **Applies to:** All metals	The wax was perfect, but the cast object has tiny pits on the surface.	Wax may not have properly burned out, the metal may have been too hot or there were impurities in the alloy.	If the problem is slight, fill the pit with hard solder and emery back. If there are lots of pits, return the piece to the casting company.
FINS DOWN SIDE OF CUTTLEFISH CAST **Applies to:** All metals	Metal has escaped from the mould.	Both halves of the mould are not meeting properly.	Re-sand both sides carefully to tighten the fit.
CUTTLEFISH CASTING UNEVEN **Applies to:** All metals	The top and bottom halves are out of alignment.	The mould has come out of registration; it might need to be remade.	Reinsert the master object, making sure that there is no movement between the halves. Re-mark the registration lines and insert registration rods, using new locations from any previous rods.
CUTTLEFISH CASTING INCOMPLETE **Applies to:** All metals	There is a part missing on the cast object.	Not enough metal has been used; it has solidified before reaching the end; or the vents for letting gas escape are inadequate.	Use more metal on the next casting.
			Make sure the pouring gate is wide enough at the bottom. Make sure the metal is hot enough when being poured.
CUTTLEFISH NOT THICK ENOUGH **Applies to:** Cuttlefish bones	If pressed into the bone, the piece would poke out of the top.	There is a limit to the height that can be cast. There must be enough material at the top and bottom of the mould.	Use two cuttlefish bones, flattening one half of each until there is enough space for the object and registration rods.

SEE: 'Best Practice: Casting Techniques', page 138, for instructions on how to make and clean up metal castings.

MOULD MAKING

PROBLEM	DESCRIPTION	CAUSES	FIX BY
BUBBLES IN SILICONE MOULD **Applies to:** Silicone	Silicone looks like a milkshake with lots of tiny bubbles.	Bubbles introduced when the silicone was mixed.	Always mix the catalyst in gently – don't beat it.
			It is worth pouring some wax in anyway, as the bubbles may only be on the top surface of the mould. If not, remake the mould.
	Random bubbles in silicone.	When pouring the rubber, a bubble has become trapped.	Pour the wax in anyway, to see if the resulting bulge might be easy to remove. If not, remake the mould.
SILICONE HAS NOT HARDENED **Applies to:** Silicone	Silicone is still very soft and tacky.	Atmospheric conditions in the workshop might have affected the curing.	Leave it another 24 hours and check again.
		The ratio of catalyst required has been miscalculated.	Check that scales are accurate and check your arithmetic.
		Make sure that the silicone is still within its use-by date.	Silicone does deteriorate over time.
INCORRECT QUANTITY OF SILICONE **Applies to:** Silicone	The object should be covered by about 2.5cm (1in) of silicone.	It is hard to estimate how much to mix, but it is better to overestimate than not have enough.	If you have made too little, quickly mix up some more and pour it on.
			If you have made too much, leave the excess in the jug or bowl. It can be pulled out in one piece when it has cured.
HORIZONTAL LINES IN VULCANISED MOULD OR INCOMPLETE MOULDING **Applies to:** Vulcanised rubber	Horizontal lines where rubber layers have not bonded.	The rubber has been packed too loosely, the surface of the rubber may have become contaminated, the vulcaniser may not have reached the correct temperature or the mould was not left in for long enough.	Remake the mould. Check that the vulcaniser is set to the correct temperature.
	Rubber has not flowed into all the cavities, so the moulding is incomplete.	Not enough rubber has been packed into the mould.	Remake the mould, pushing small scraps of rubber into every area, and adding one extra layer on top.
BUBBLES IN VULCANISED MOULD **Applies to:** Vulcanised rubber	The rubber looks like it has boiled.	The vulcaniser is too hot.	Remake the mould, making sure that the vulcaniser is set to the temperature recommended by the rubber manufacturer.

Continued overleaf

SHAPING

DECORATION

WIREWORK

CASTING

STONE SETTING

Casting continued

PROBLEM	DESCRIPTION	CAUSES	FIX BY
VULCANISED MOULD CURLING UP **Applies to:** Vulcanised rubber	Curling mould.	This sometimes happens with pink moulding rubber.	Place a weight on it overnight to try to remove the curl.
			Remould using white rubber on the top and bottom few layers.
SOLDERED PARTS OF THE MASTER ARE MELTING WHEN ATTACHING A SPRUE **Applies to:** All metals	The master piece is falling apart.	The master has been exposed to too much heat.	Protect existing solder joints with heat-resistant paste or gel. Use easy solder or paste to attach the sprue.
SPRUE DETACHED FROM OBJECT **Applies to:** Vulcanised moulds	Rubber has flowed into the gap.	The pressure of the vulcaniser has caused the weak solder joint to fail.	Cut a channel in the rubber where the sprue should have been. If that fails, remake the mould.
VULCANISED MOULD HARD TO CUT OPEN **Applies to:** Vulcanised rubber	The rubber is very springy.	The model has been overpacked.	Warm the mould slightly before cutting it. Use a new scalpel and dip it regularly into a solution of liquid detergent and water. Support the mould in a vice to free up both hands.
WAX HAS NOT REACHED END OF VULCANISED MOULD **Applies to:** Vulcanised moulds	The resulting model is incomplete.	Not enough wax has been injected.	Inject for longer next time.
		Wax solidified before reaching the end of the mould.	Warm the mould slightly.
WAX CASTING SNAPS WHEN BEING REMOVED **Applies to:** Wax castings	Impossible to get a whole wax from the mould.	Wax has cooled and become brittle.	Open up more quickly next time, and straighten out the wax while it is still malleable.
		One area may be trapped and hard to remove.	Cut the mould to make it easier to extract.
FAULT IN EVERY WAX **Applies to:** Wax castings	Every wax is identically imperfect.	There may be a fault in the master or the mould may be contaminated.	Check the master. Look at the wax and decide if the fault can be easily removed after casting. If not, remake the mould.
WAX HAS ESCAPED FROM INJECTED MOULD **Applies to:** Wax castings	There are large fins down the side of the wax.	This is flashing caused by wax being forced into the parting line of the mould.	Reduce the air pressure on the injector.
			Hold the sides of the mould together firmly when injecting it.
AIR BUBBLES IN THE INJECTED WAX **Applies to:** Wax castings	Wax model is not smooth.	Wax is at the wrong temperature, it may be running out or the air pressure may be too high.	Check the injection machine to get the right pressure, temperature and wax level.
		Air may have been introduced via the nozzle.	Make sure that the mould is firmly pressed against the nozzle when injecting.

SEE: 'Best Practice: Mould Making', page 142, for how to make silicone and rubber moulds, and how to use them to create wax models for casting.

Stone Setting

BEZEL SETTING

PROBLEM	DESCRIPTION	CAUSES	FIX BY
STONE TOO LARGE Applies to: Bezel settings	Despite using some force, the stone will not go into the bezel.	The bezel was too small and was then soldered in place, making resizing difficult.	Try running a burnisher around the bezel, or a riffler file around the base of the bezel. Make sure the stone is sitting flat when put into the setting.
			You might need to remake the setting with a larger bezel if the above options do not work.
STONE TOO SMALL Applies to: Bezel settings	The stone is moving from side to side or is rotating in the setting.	The bezel is too big for the stone.	The setting will have to be remade.
STONE HAS FALLEN OUT Applies to: Bezel settings	During the setting procedure, stones sometimes ping out.	The stone was not sitting properly in the bezel. The bezel may be too tight for the stone.	Try opening it with a burnisher.
		It may be too short for the stone.	The setting will have to be remade.
STONE IS JAMMED Applies to: Bezel settings	It clicked into place and cannot be removed.	If the setting is quite tight, it can be very hard to grab the smooth curved surface of the stone.	Use a small cone of beeswax to pull the stone out sharply.
			Drill a small hole on the underside of the bezel and push the stone out.
SETTING HAS COME OFF RING Applies to: Bezel settings	A common problem when making rings.	The solder joint was not strong enough to stand the pressure of setting.	Try to remove the stone by running a scribe between the bezel and the stone, and then re-solder the setting on.
			Carefully saw the stone out of the setting and remake it.
GAP AT BASE OF BEZEL Applies to: Bezel settings	Hole enlarges as the stone is set.	Solder did not flow all around the joint.	Saw out the stone and make another bezel.
BEZEL WALLS DON'T MEET STONE Applies to: Bezel settings	There is a gap around the top of the bezel.	The bezel is too thick or has not been pushed over far enough.	Run a flat needle file around the very top of the outside of the setting at a 45-degree angle to thin the edge for pushing over.
			If using a very heavy bezel, anneal it before setting.
			Use a chasing tool and hammer to push the setting over.

Continued overleaf

SHAPING

DECORATION

WIREWORK

CASTING

STONE SETTING

Stone Setting continued

PROBLEM	DESCRIPTION	CAUSES	FIX BY
STONE MOVES **Applies to:** Bezel settings	When one side is pushed over, the stone tilts.	The base of the stone is not flat.	Make a jump ring of the appropriate size and solder it into the base of the bezel.
PUSH TOOL SLIPS **Applies to:** Bezel settings	Impossible to apply adequate pressure without the tool slipping.	Polished push tools leave no marks on the metal, but can easily slip.	Key a slight texture on the push tool with a file. Sand off any marks left on the setting afterwards.
CORNERS TOO LONG **Applies to:** Square bezel settings	Excess metal is appearing at the corners of the stone.	Bezel is too large and too thin.	Try filing off the excess metal at the corners.
			Remake more accurately and of slightly thicker gauge metal.
STONE TOO DEEP OR NOT STRAIGHT IN TUBE **Applies to:** Tube settings	The stone is too deep and is being obscured by the metal.	The setting burr has been pushed too far down the tube.	Remove the stone. File off some metal from the top of the setting, then re-burr carefully using a setting burr.
	A stone that sits askew in the tube is particularly noticeable on faceted stones.	The seat the stone is resting on is not straight.	As above, making sure that re-burring is straight.
TUBE TOO THICK **Applies to:** Tube settings	Tube too thick for the stone.	There is too much metal to push over without unseating the stone.	File the top of the tube to a 45-degree angle. Anneal it before setting.

SEE: 'Best Practice: Bezel Setting', page 156, for advice on making a bezel from sheet metal or tube to set a stone.

FLUSH AND PRONG SETTING

PROBLEM	DESCRIPTION	CAUSES	FIX BY
STONE HAS FALLEN OUT OF FLUSH SETTING **Applies to:** Flush settings	Stone falls out when upended or pulled with beeswax.	The seat is too shallow.	Return the stone to the setting and check the depth. Re-burr deeper.
		The burr was too large.	Anneal the setting and use more pressure when inserting the stone.
			Try to find a slightly larger stone.
STONE TOO DEEP IN FLUSH SETTING **Applies to:** Flush settings	It is hard to see the stone in a recess.	The setting burr went too deep.	File and emery the area around the stone.
			Drill the setting out, solder a piece of wire into the hole and then reset the stone.

PROBLEM	DESCRIPTION	CAUSES	FIX BY
SCRATCHES ON FLUSH SETTING OR STONE **Applies to:** Flush settings	The area around the stone is scratched rather than smooth.	The setting tool may be too sharp.	Check the tool is blunt and polished.
		The tool may have slipped.	Rub the scratches with a polished burnisher.
	A chip or scratch has appeared on the stone.	Some stones are too soft to withstand the force of the steel tool when flush setting.	Flush setting is not recommended for stones below 8 on the Mohs hardness scale. Try to find a harder stone.
JUMP RINGS ON PRONG SETTING NOT PARALLEL **Applies to:** Prong settings	The setting looks crooked.	One or both of the jump rings may have slipped when being soldered.	De-solder the jump ring or rings. Pickle, rinse and re-solder.
PRONG HAS MELTED **Applies to:** Prong settings	Melted prong.	While soldering one part, another has melted.	Put the stone in and see if the damaged part can be cut off.
			Remake the setting if necessary, keeping a close eye on the torch flame when soldering.
HARD TO SAW WIRE OUT OF V SECTION **Applies to:** Prong settings	Cutting the space for the second set of prongs is difficult.	Wire keeps springing about and is hard to saw.	Grip the wire in parallel pliers and use these to guide the saw.
LARGER JUMP RING NOT SITTING STRAIGHT **Applies to:** Prong settings	The jump ring keeps moving.	The prongs are too splayed out.	Squeeze the wires together a bit so that they support the jump ring.
		The notches in the jump ring are too shallow.	Increase the depth of the notches with a gapping or needle file.
PRONGS LOOK BULGY AND DON'T HOLD STONE **Applies to:** Prong settings	Setting does not look crisp.	The nick in the prongs where the girdle sits might be at the wrong height or too shallow.	Straighten the prongs and re-burr.
		The prongs may be too thick.	Remove the stone, straighten the jump rings and file them. Anneal the setting lightly before resetting the stone.
		The seating jump ring may be too large or small.	If too small, lose some of the prong width from the inside edge of the setting. If too large, the setting will have to be remade.

SEE: 'Best Practice: Flush and Prong Setting', page 160, for guidance on setting stones flush with a piece or raising them in a pronged mount.

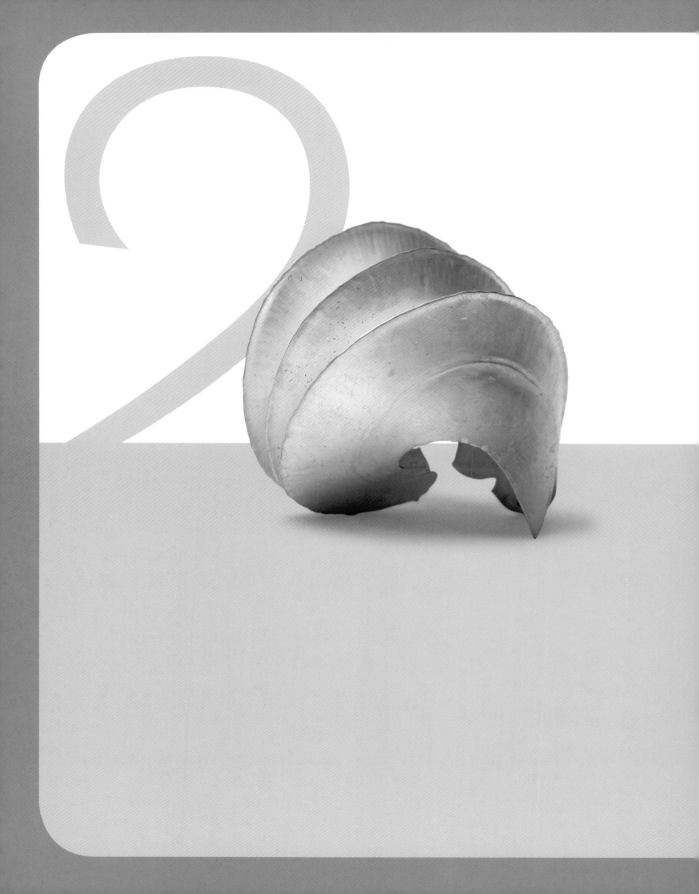

CHAPTER 2

SHAPING

Cutting metal with a piercing saw is the first stage in the making process. Establishing good technique in this fundamental skill will save you time and energy, and will result in pieces that have a fluent rather than a laboured appearance. After being cut, rhythm, form and volume can be given to the piece by bending, forging and soldering it – thus transforming it from the sum of its component parts into a stunning piece of jewellery.

Cutting and piercing

A jewellery saw, also known as a piercing saw, is the most common tool used to cut or pierce metal. Larger pieces of metal can be cut with a guillotine or shears, although either of these will slightly compromise the edge of the metal, so are not suitable for accurate cutting.

▲ KATE CASE

Beautifully intricate pieces such as this pendant can be made given patience, practice and plenty of saw blades.

The advantage of a piercing saw is that it is relatively cheap, portable and low tech. With practice (and patience) the most intricate and sophisticated work can be created with the humble piercing saw.

There are a few fundamental steps to achieving a good result when using a piercing saw to cut metal. The most important points to remember are to relax, don't rush and constantly observe what the saw is doing.

Different metals handle differently when cut (see chart, right). If working with precious metals, make sure that you collect the valuable dust or filings, which can be recycled by a metal dealer.

Selecting and attaching a blade

You should select the best saw blade for the thickness of metal. Hold the blade against the edge of the piece of metal to be cut – more than two, but not more than three, saw blade teeth should be touching the metal. Saw blade sizes run from 6 (thickest) to 8/0 (finest). A very useful general size for cutting metal of around 18 gauge (1mm) is 2/0.

Make sure that you attach the blade to the frame correctly. Hold the blade with teeth facing upwards. The teeth should be pointing towards the handle of the saw. Bear in mind that the action stroke with a saw is always the downward stroke, so the blade should feel rough when stroked from the handle to the end of the frame.

Tighten the screw nearest the handle, then while pushing the top end of the frame against the bench peg, tighten the top screw. This compresses the frame and adds tension to the blade, which should 'ping' musically when plucked. If the sound it makes is too high, the tension is too tight and it will be prone to snapping.

METAL	CHARACTERISTICS WHEN CUTTING
Copper	▪ Feels fairly open-grained. ▪ An excellent metal to practise piercing with. ▪ As it is cut, the dust falls in relatively large particles.
Brass	▪ Similar to copper but feels slightly coarser. ▪ When sawing, catch the dust in a clean tray or bench skin to keep separate from any precious metal dust.
Aluminium	▪ Feels grainier and lighter than copper or brass. ▪ Keep saw blades separate from those used for other metals because the dust would contaminate them during any heating or soldering operations.
Stainless steel	▪ Feels quite close-grained and very hard. ▪ Sawing takes much longer than for other metals and the saw blades may wear out fairly quickly.
Standard silver	▪ Has quite a close grain and is very soft, making it easy to cut, but it will bend as you are cutting. ▪ Dust can be collected in the bench skin and saved to sell with other scrap pieces.
Low-carat gold	▪ The major part of a low-carat gold is a mixture of non-gold metals, so it feels slightly coarser than silver but is not difficult to cut. ▪ Gold dust from cutting should be kept separately, so clean the bench skin before you start.
High-carat gold	▪ Has a close-grain feel about it and cuts beautifully. ▪ All gold dust should be stored carefully according to carat levels.

Preparing the work

The next important consideration is the peg on which the metal will be supported while it is cut. It should extend out from the top of the bench and should be horizontal and firm. Some people remove the sloping bench peg that they use for filing and turn it upside down to present a flat support for piercing. The shape to be cut should be accurately transferred to the metal. The easiest way to do this is to attach a drawing, computer printout or photocopy to the metal with double-sided tape. Outlines can also be transferred with carbon paper, drawn with a fine permanent pen or scratched onto the metal with a scribe.

9cm (3½in)

12.5cm (5in)

▲ Template for a saw peg.

Cutting technique

With the metal flat on the peg, decide where the first cut should be and run the saw blade up the edge of the piece from the top of the saw frame to the handle — this should make a small groove for the first proper stroke of the saw to sit in.

Holding the saw Hold the handle of the saw loosely and move the frame up and down gently. The cutting action should be smooth, with no tension in the cutting hand. Relax and don't push on the saw blade — it is designed to 'bite' the metal on its own and will do most of the work for you. Try to keep the saw at 90 degrees to the metal at all times, so that whatever happens on the top of the piece is repeated on the underside. Always hold the metal flat to the peg with the non-sawing hand.

Turning corners When turning a corner, make sure that you keep the saw blade moving up and down to prevent the blade from twisting. When sawing an acute angle, it is sometimes useful to pull back slightly using the smooth back edge of the saw blade to pivot on. It is good practice to saw very slightly outside the line, so that the edge of the original drawing is still visible. This line can then be used as a guide to file back to, giving a perfect result. If the line is crossed, the areas on either side of the error have to be filed back, and this can be a problem if the piece is a perfect circle or a very symmetrical shape. It is easier to correct a little 'mountain' that can be filed off, than a valley that must be filed down to.

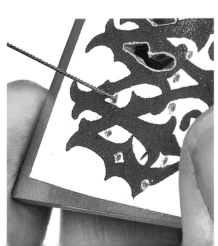

▲ On acute angles, use the smooth back of the saw blade to allow the saw teeth to pivot around without twisting.

Cutting internal shapes
To pierce out internal shapes, a small hole must be drilled to allow the saw blade to be inserted. Drill the hole near the edge to be cut, but not so near that it creates a notch in it. Release the top end of the saw blade and thread the metal on to it, making sure the pattern to be cut is facing upwards. Pierce out the shape. It is best to pierce out all the internal shapes in a piece before cutting around the outside.

◀ Keep the saw blade perpendicular to the work and don't exert any force on it.

▶ To cut internal shapes, thread the blade through from the back to the front so that it will be the correct way round.

WHAT'S THE PROBLEM?

SHAPING

DECORATION

WIREWORK

CASTING

STONE SETTING

Filing

Files are used to remove saw blade marks or excess solder from metal and to refine and shape materials. Files come in numerous profiles and various grades of roughness. Choosing the correct file for the job and using it properly can save lots of time and result in a beautifully finished object.

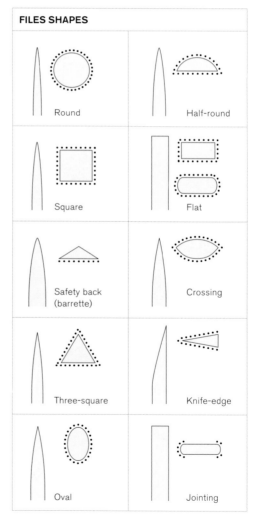

Files come in different grades – the roughest is a cut 00 and is generally used to roughly file down sprues or large edges. In most jewellery applications a cut 00 file would make more marks than it removes. The smoothest files are cut 6. For general usage a cut 0 half-round file and a selection of cut 2 files are most useful. A set of 12 cut 2 or 4 needle files is good for fine work.

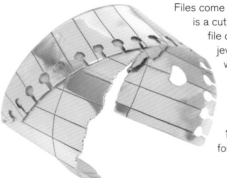

▲ ZORAH RAHMAN
This pierced and engraved cuff uses accurate finishing to imitate torn paper in silver.

Selecting the right file

As a general rule, use the largest file you can for a job – there is no point in trying to straighten a long edge with a needle file. Having a mid-grade file is most useful (cut 2); you can imitate a higher grade of file by wrapping a sheet of emery paper around the file for a finer finish. If you can only afford one file initially, get a half-round file so that you will have a flat face and a curved one available. Bear in mind that most files are rough all around and it is easy to accidentally file using the back of the file – one safety back, or barrette, needle file is a good investment.

Attaching a handle

Most files have a tapered tang for the fitting of a wooden handle, which makes their use more efficient. A handle means the effective stroke of the file is extended and it is more comfortable to use. If your handle does not already have a hole in it, drill one that is half the diameter of the widest part of the tang. Keeping both handle and file straight, insert the handle and deliver a couple of firm blows with a wooden mallet on a sturdy surface (or in a vice).

FILES SHAPES	
Round	Half-round
Square	Flat
Safety back (barrette)	Crossing
Three-square	Knife-edge
Oval	Jointing

Hold the work in a vice if necessary.

▲ Keep your wrist action fluid when filing curved forms.

What to file on

Filing should always be done with the work supported on a firm surface. The classic sloping bench peg on the centre of a jeweller's bench is designed for filing; the slope means that the work can be easily observed while being filed. The edge of a saw peg can be employed to keep straight lines parallel. If the shape allows, work can be held in a vice; use safe jaws to protect the metal surface and check regularly that the metal has not slipped in the jaws.

Filing technique

The profile of the file you choose should correspond most closely to the shape of the object being filed: flat files for straight edges and convex curves, and half-round or round files for concave curves. The whole width of the file should make contact with the piece. Hold the piece firmly while resting it on the bench peg. The forward stroke of the file is the cutting stroke; use the back stroke to reposition the file.

▼ Hold the piece firmly with the non-filing hand.

When filing curved forms, such as the outside of a ring shank, remember to keep your wrist movement fluid to avoid flattening out the profile. Conversely, when filing a straight edge be careful to keep the whole length of the stroke straight – it is very easy to slope down at the beginning and end of a straight line. Check constantly that you are achieving the right shape with your filing.

Cleaning and caring for files

Sometimes files can become clogged with dust. Use a file brush to clean them, or run the edge of a scrap of copper sheet along the file at a 45-degree angle. Ideally files should not just be thrown in a drawer or toolbox because they will become damaged by rubbing together. Separate them with a cloth, or hang on a magnetic strip in the workshop.

After filing

Once a piece has been filed to your satisfaction, remove any file marks by working up the grades of emery paper. These abrasive sheets come in grades from rough (150) to very smooth (1200). Generally, working through four grades – 400, 600, 800 and 1000 – is sufficient to get a good finish on jewellery.

Sheets of abrasive paper can be fixed to a sheet of glass for smoothing flat pieces; they can be wrapped around files for more complex areas or taped to wooden sticks (buff sticks); and they can be torn into strips or rolled up to reach into small areas.

SHAPING

DECORATION

WIREWORK

CASTING

STONE SETTING

Annealing

Metals tend to be hard due to their crystalline structure. Annealing metals by heating relaxes them, making them softer, pliable and capable of being worked.

In order to achieve smooth curves it is necessary to anneal metal before bending it. This makes the task easier and prevents having to use excess force. As the metal is worked, it will regain its hardness and need to be re-annealed. Complex or large forms can be re-annealed many times in their construction. With practice, the jeweller will know when to re-anneal by the feel and sound of the metal.

▲ RALPH BAKKER
The gold earhooks have been annealed to lend them fluidity and are juxtaposed against black enamelled pieces.

Hearth and torches

It is worth investing in a soldering stand and a selection of heatproof mats and soldering blocks of various dimensions so that you can construct walls to reflect the heat back when annealing thick or large objects. The hearth area should be well insulated and should be regularly cleaned to prevent any contamination or small pieces of solder from attaching to the metal. Make sure the lighting is not too bright around the hearth so that the changes of colour can be easily observed. Keep a fire extinguisher and a bowl of water within easy reach.

Most people start making jewellery with a portable hand torch. It is possible to anneal small pieces with such a torch, but because they are quite weak, it is advisable to build a little box structure from firebricks to maximise the heat getting to the object. An atmospheric torch will have more power. These use pressurised canisters of propane, butane or acetylene and draw oxygen from the air. When choosing a hand torch, it is a good idea to try as many as you can to see which feels the most comfortable and easy to use.

ANNEALING TEMPERATURES FOR DIFFERENT METALS

Metal	Temperature		Colour	Cooling method
Copper	750–1200°F	400–650°C	Dark red	Quench in cold water
Brass	840–1350°F	450–730°C	Dull red	Allow to air cool
Gilding metal	840–1300°F	450–700°C	Dull red	Quench in cold water
Steel	1500–1650°F	800–900°C	Cherry red	Quench in cold water
Sterling silver	1200°F	650°C	Dull red	Quench in cold water when metal has cooled to black heat
Yellow gold	1200–1300°F	650–700°C	Dull red	Quench in cold water when metal has cooled to black heat
White gold	1400°F	750°C	Dull red	Quench in cold water when metal has cooled to black heat
Red gold	1200°F	650°C	Dull red	Quench above 500°C (930°F)
Platinum	1850°F	1000°C	Orange-yellow	Allow to air cool
Palladium	1500–1650°F	800–900°C	Yellow-orange	Quench in cold water when metal has cooled to black heat

WHAT'S THE PROBLEM?

SHAPING

DECORATION

WIREWORK

CASTING

STONE SETTING

▲ Torch is too close
to heat effectively.

▲ Move torch back to focus the heat.

▲ Annealing is achieved when the metal reaches
the appropriate uniform colour (here, orange).

How to anneal

It is important to know where the hottest point of the torch flame is – generally just beyond the blue cone. You can test this by pointing the flame at a fireproof mat. If there is a glowing halo shape with a colourless centre, the flame needs to be moved farther away until a glowing circle appears.

Place the metal on a clean heatproof mat and heat with a soft bushy flame until the metal glows dull red. Move the torch slowly and evenly over the metal until a uniform red glow is achieved. Hold this colour for a couple of seconds. Quench the metal in water, or allow to air cool in the case of brass or platinum.

When annealing wire it is best to wrap it into a tight coil, carefully winding the ends around the coil to secure it. Keep the flame moving around the coil, heating it evenly; any exposed strands of wire will be easily melted. Turn the coil over with tweezers and heat the other side.

Pickling

When metal is heated a chemical reaction takes place, resulting in oxides being deposited on the surface of the metal. These can be removed in a mildly acidic solution known as pickle. Traditionally a solution of 1 part sulphuric acid to 9 parts water was used as pickle. Now it is possible to buy pickling powder or safety pickle from jewellery suppliers. Despite the name, care should be taken when handling it and it should be used in a well-ventilated area.

Pickle powder is diluted in water and works best when gently heated. Most commercial jewellers and colleges will have a pickling unit that keeps the pickle warm. In the home workshop a plastic tub of pickle placed in a slow cooker of water is a good alternative. It is important to remember to switch it off after use – a timer on a plug is a good idea.

Never use steel tweezers to remove work from the pickling solution – an electro-chemical reaction will occur, causing molecules of copper to be deposited on the surface of silver, turning it pink. This must then be reheated and pickled repeatedly or abraded to remove the copper.

Hollow forms may get pickle trapped inside them. This should be removed by squirting clean water in via a syringe. Pieces can also be soaked in a solution of bicarbonate of soda, which will neutralise the acid. Bicarbonate of soda (or soda ash) can also be used to neutralise the pickle prior to disposal. It is also possible to pickle metal with vinegar and salt or lemon juice, or with a solution of alum.

▲ Use stainless steel, brass or plastic tweezers to transfer items to and from the pickle.

▲ Remove the metal when it is clean (usually about 5 minutes) – it should be matt white.

Ring bending

Most rings have a shank of bent sheet or wire. An easy way to make a ring shank is to bend the metal into a spiral shape prior to sawing to size, or you can calculate the exact length of metal to bend into shape if the material is particularly expensive or scarce.

Bending a simple band ring

Cut a strip of metal to the required width for the ring, allowing about 7cm (2¾in) in length. Anneal and pickle the metal to be made into the ring shank.

▲ STEPHANIE JOHNSON
This folded ring exploits the contrast between the textured surface and the burnished edge of the metal.

1 Bend the metal into a round shape using half-round pliers, with the rounded arm of the pliers forming the inside of the ring. Keep winding until it forms a spiral, or in the case of wire until the two ends move past each other. This could also be done on a ring mandrel.

3 Place the spiral on the edge of the saw peg and saw through the middle where the two ends cross over. Hold the piece very firmly and don't stop sawing until both ends have been cut off.

2 Check the size using a ring sizer or finger. Make the ring larger on the mandrel if necessary. Remember that it is easier to make a ring slightly larger than smaller. Don't worry if it is not circular at this point.

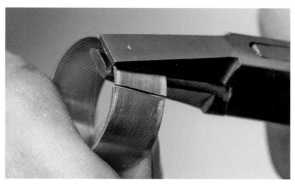

4 Manipulate the ends back and forth with ring pliers until they meet perfectly. Push one end behind the other, turn over and repeat until they fit together with some tension.

WHAT'S THE PROBLEM?

SHAPING

DECORATION

WIREWORK

CASTING

STONE SETTING

Calculating exact length of metal

To cut the precise length of metal required, refer to the chart on page 170, remembering to add on 1.5 times the thickness of the metal to the ring's length – that is, a size 8 ring would require 60.9mm plus 1.5mm if being made in 1mm (18-gauge) metal. Cut to the correct length, anneal and bend until the edges meet perfectly. Solder, then true up on the mandrel.

Piercing a ring blank

Interest can be added to a band ring by piercing out patterns or shapes, but a couple of rules should be followed when doing this. Don't pierce out too much material or the ring will be very hard to bend, and don't pierce too close to the edge. If you are using text, remember that the middle of letters such as R and A will fall out when pierced. Straight lines can be very effective, but require accurate piercing and finishing.

1 Attach a drawing to the metal using double-sided tape.

2 Drill holes for the saw blade to go through for piercing out the internal shapes.

3 Insert the saw blade, pierce out the shapes and then saw around the outside of the drawing. The ring is now ready to be annealed, bent and soldered.

5 The ring is now ready to solder the ends together.

6 Once it has been soldered, place the ring back on to the mandrel and use a mallet to perfect the round shape.

▲ The finished ring with flush-set stones.

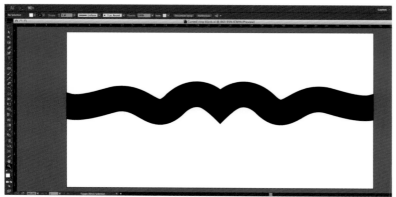
▲ Design for shaped band ring.

Shaped band rings

The edge of a band ring does not have to be straight – there are plenty of options for adding detail, as long as you make sure that the ends meet up seamlessly. Drawing out the pattern on squared paper is helpful, or design it using a software drawing package with guides to line up the ends.

▲ Piercing the ring.

▲ The finished ring.

Textured finishes

With the exception of hammer finishes, texture is best added to a ring before it is fabricated. Textured rings are best soldered from the inside of the shank, and care should be taken that the texture is not fluxed or the solder is liable to flow into it. Often the texture can be imitated over the solder line with the use of various burrs on a micromotor or needle files.

Percussive finishes can be added to a finished ring on a triblet using creasing or ball-peen hammers or decorative punches. This will result in the ring stretching and becoming thinner; depending on the frequency of the blows, the ring can end up considerably larger than it started. This should be allowed for by making the ring using a thicker gauge of metal and smaller than required.

◄ Hammer-textured ring

WHAT'S THE PROBLEM?

SHAPING

DECORATION

WIREWORK

CASTING

STONE SETTING

Forging

Forging is an ancient technique for forming and shaping metal using hammers and stakes. It exploits the plastic nature of annealed metal and can result in surprisingly complex and sculptural forms that tend to have an organic appearance.

▶ PHILIP SAJET
The forged nail adds movement to the earrings.

Hammers and stakes

The direction in which the metal moves during forging is dictated by the shape of the hammer head. A flat striking face, such as a planishing hammer, will have relatively little effect on metal as the force will be distributed over a large area, but it is very useful for fine finishing. A convex (crowned) striking face will push the metal outwards in all directions around a concentrated point of impact, resulting in greater deformation – the more domed the hammer (such as a ball-peen hammer), the more metal will be moved, but more marks will be deposited on it. A wedge-shaped striking face, such as a cross-peen hammer, will exert force downwards and perpendicular on the metal. This hammer allows lots of control in the direction of the deformation and is good for rapid forging.

The stake provides a hard resistant surface to support metal while it is being worked, and selecting the best stake for the job is important to the final outcome. Forging on a curved stake will force the metal out from the point of contact, exaggerating the effect of the hammer. A small bench anvil provides a variety of useful curved and flat surfaces. A tree stump can provide a multitude of indentations for doming and holes for stakes, and provides a surface for invasive work that is not too precious. A flat steel plate is essential for the beginner.

▲ Flat striking face

▲ Convex striking face

Set-up

Always make sure that the piece you are working on is at a comfortable height – it should be at the same height as your elbow. Hold the hammer at the end of the handle; it is an extension of your arm and the stroke will be more powerful pivoted from the elbow rather than the wrist. Forging is noisy, so consider wearing ear protection. Also wear sturdy shoes in case you drop a hammer or stake.

▲ Wedge-shaped striking face

▼ Selection of stakes

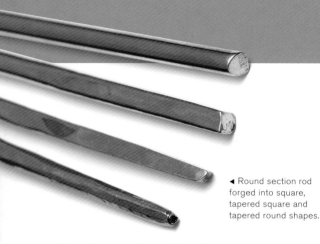

Forging to square up or taper rod

On a steel stake use a raising hammer to flatten one face of the rod. Turn 90 degrees and repeat. Keep turning and forging until the desired width/length is achieved; to create a taper, concentrate more on the tip of the rod. To make the rod into round section, rotate 45 degrees and forge the corners off the square section. Keep turning the rod and hit with successively lighter strokes as section becomes round. Pay attention to the feel and sound of the metal – when it starts to feel less flexible and sounds higher pitched, it will need to be re-annealed.

◄ Round section rod forged into square, tapered square and tapered round shapes.

Forging a ring shank

Start with a 55mm length of 3mm diameter round rod. Flatten the midsection with a cross-peen hammer, then rotate 90 degrees and flatten each end to the same degree. Bend the ends in a swage block, followed by the middle section (which should bend more easily due to its relative thinness). Adjust the seam with a piercing saw to make sure the ends meet perfectly, then solder. File and sand the ring to eliminate hammer marks. The solder joint can be sawn open to allow the insertion of a prong setting. This style of ring is a useful way of holding a stone setting at a reasonable height.

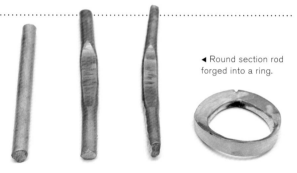

◄ Round section rod forged into a ring.

Fold forming

Folding and hammering sheet metal can result in dramatic sculptural forms that are relatively light. The sheet metal should not be too thick as this can make the resulting forms heavy and hard to open, so use metal of around 0.4mm (26 gauge). Using copper for initial experiments will keep the costs down, and making detailed notes of shapes and

dimensions used should help with progress in this area. Avoid pickling the metals between annealing as this may cause them to fuse when reheated. These forms respond well to patination and barrel polishing to emphasise their sculptural nature.

Double folded form

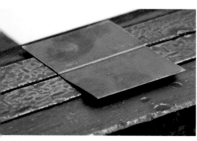

1 Fold a piece of 0.4mm sheet metal in half. Position the folded edge in a vice and open it out.

2 Fold it back on itself to create an M shape. Insert the folded side into the vice and open out as before. Remove from the vice and trim the legs of the M.

3 Use a creasing hammer to forge just inside the edge of the fold. Anneal regularly (but don't pickle) and keep forging until the desired curvature is reached.

4 Anneal, then pry open the piece with a blunt knife to reveal the double folded form.

WHAT'S THE PROBLEM?

SHAPING

DECORATION

WIREWORK

CASTING

STONE SETTING

Single fold using a shim

1 Fold a piece of 0.4mm thick sheet metal in half and insert a 1mm thick strip of copper along the fold seam. Close the strip in a vice and hammer the shim tightly into place. With a guillotine or tin snips, cut the piece to shape.

2 Pass it through a rolling mill with the ends at 90 degrees to the rollers. Repeat several times and anneal as necessary, but do not pickle. Repeat until the folded edge is the same thickness as the rest of the metal.

3 Anneal again and then pry the form open with a blunt knife or wooden wedge. Remove the shim and then manipulate by hand into the desired shape. Pickle.

Anticlastic raising

Anticlastic raising enables concave curves to be created using a curved hammer on a curved stake. For most anticlastic raising a sinusoidal stake is required. This is essentially a tapered triblet that has been bent into a wiggly snake-like former, resulting in an assortment of curves that can be used to form metal when struck with a wedge-shaped mallet. As with all forging, experimentation is key – given the variables of metal thickness and shapes and curves available on the stake, it is worth keeping detailed notes and charting the progress of the raising. Raising closed forms is easier as they are the most readily controlled, but open shapes raised from fairly thin metal (0.6mm/22 gauge) can result in strong, lightweight sculptural forms.

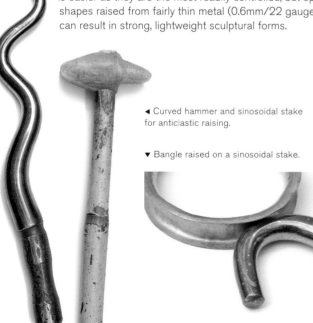

◄ Curved hammer and sinosoidal stake for anticlastic raising.

▼ Bangle raised on a sinosoidal stake.

Raising a ring using punches

1 With small objects such as rings, an anticlastic effect can be obtained by stretching the ring between two round punches. Secure one punch upright in a vice, balance the ring on top and then hold another punch on top of the ring. It is important that the punches do not touch each other.

2 Keeping them absolutely vertical, hit the top punch with a hammer or mallet. Anneal regularly. Remember that rings should not be raised too far in this manner because they become uncomfortable to wear.

Doming and swaging

Doming and swaging require special blocks and punches, which are very useful in that they can produce easily replicated identical elements. If you care for them well, they should last a lifetime.

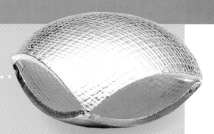

▲ Shapes other than circles can be domed to interesting effect.

Doming blocks, also known as dapping blocks, can either be large rectangular steel blocks or smaller cube-shaped blocks in brass or wood, with hemispherical depressions of decreasing sizes. The corresponding punches are made of steel or wood, and are used to form metals into a regular domed shape. Discs can be domed up to make spherical forms, but any shape that fits in the block can be domed. Care should be taken to preserve any texture that has been applied to the metal with a small piece of tissue paper when forming, as the punches will tend to knock this out.

Swage blocks are useful for bending up long pieces of metal when this cannot be done with pliers. They are also used for making tube to specific dimensions, which can be very useful for constructing brooch fastenings or tube setting stones.

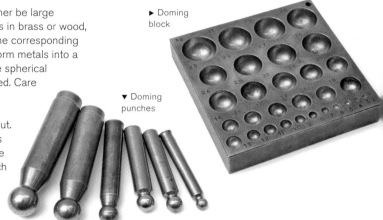

▶ Doming block

▼ Doming punches

Creating a sphere

Decide how big you would like the sphere to be. As a general rule of thumb this is the desired finished diameter plus the height of the dome, though it is hard to estimate exactly as the metal does stretch somewhat on being domed. Use a compass, scribe around a template or attach a printed image to the metal with double-sided tape. Pierce out the disc and finish the edge with a needle file. Anneal, pickle and dry the discs ready for doming.

Doming metal discs to form a sphere

1 Place the doming block on a sandbag to decrease the noise. Select a depression in the block into which the disc fits easily – it is better to start doming gradually.

2 Select the right size of punch for the hole, making sure the punch has some leeway. If the punch is too large, it will become damaged. Hammer several times. Work down through the sizes until the required diameter is reached.

3 Sand down the edges of a pair of discs and drill a hole in one of them to allow air to escape as it expands when being soldered.

4 Secure the domed discs together with binding wire and solder together.

▲ The finished sphere.

WHAT'S THE PROBLEM?

SHAPING

DECORATION

WIREWORK

CASTING

STONE SETTING

▲ Strip of metal ready to be swaged.

▲ As the strip bends around the metal rod, move to a smaller indentation.

Tube of metal after it has been pulled through a draw plate.

Swaging a piece of tube

Tubing, or chenier, is available commercially in various wall thicknesses and sizes, but occasionally a project will require a specification that is not available. You can form the tubing yourself from a strip of metal using a swage block. Refer to the chart below to calculate the width of metal strip you will need to use.

Anneal, pickle and dry the strip to be swaged (always make a bit more than you need). Select a depression in the swage block that fits it comfortably. Place a corresponding rod of metal (or the handle of a doming punch) over the metal strip and hit with a mallet. Keep moving down the sizes of indentations in the swage block. Metal can be encouraged over the former using a soft mallet on a wooden surface, then evened up using the swage block. Once the edges are touching, cut through with a piercing saw to even up and then solder together.

Long lengths of tube can be pulled through a draw plate to true them up and stretch them to a specific width.

▲ Swage blocks can also be used to hammer round wire into D-section wire.

CALCULATING THE WIDTH OF METAL REQUIRED FOR SWAGING TUBING

To generate a specific outside diameter	Subtract the metal thickness from the outside diameter and multiply by 3.14 ([outside diameter − metal thickness] x 3.14)
To generate a specific inside diameter	Add the inside diameter to the metal thickness and multiply by 3.14 ([inside diameter + metal thickness] x 3.14)
If you know the outside and inside diameters required, the following formula will tell you the width of metal required	Outside diameter minus inside diameter divided by 2 ([outside diameter − inside diameter] ÷ 2); then to find the width of the blank: inside diameter plus metal thickness multiplied by 3.14 ([inside diameter + metal thickness] x 3.14)

Repoussage and chasing

A trip to any museum will reveal a wealth of repoussé work, dating back to the Bronze Age. Annealed metal is set in a bowl of pitch, which supports the metal while it is deformed using various punches and chasing tools. The metal can be turned over and worked repeatedly from opposite sides to create intricate undulating forms.

▲ KATE CASE
The shape for this shell brooch was cut out first and then repousséed to minimise any stretching of the metal.

There are various recipes for making the pitch used in repoussé work. Pitch (a form of asphalt) on its own is too soft for repoussage, so it has to be bulked out with fillers to give the right degree of resistance. These can be brick dust, plaster of Paris or pumice, and are added gently to the melted pitch. Emollients are used to soften the pitch; these can be oil, tallow or resin. Experimentation with these elements should result in the perfect pitch, although the formula may need to be seasonally adjusted as it will get softer in summer and harder in winter. It is also available ready-made from some jewellery suppliers.

The pitch is usually contained in a round pitch bowl set upon a rubber or basket base so that the work can be easily tilted. The pitch bowl is quite heavy, so wear sturdy shoes when chasing.

Punches and hammers

Doming punches and commercially available chasing punches can be used. If you have access to a grinder, making your own set of custom punches from tool steel is a good idea. All edges should be softened to prevent the metal from splitting, and the faces should be highly polished to allow them to move smoothly. Punches will have to be tempered before use to make them durable – slowly heat from the non-business end of the tool. The colour should change from pale straw yellow through dark brown/bronze then into purple/blue. This is when you should stop to achieve the right strength for a chasing tool – quench immediately in cold water.

Repoussé hammers have a large round face and a handle that is skinny at the top and fat and curved at the bottom. The large face means that you can concentrate on the end of the chasing tool, rather than having to focus on where the hammer is hitting. The thin shaft of the hammer allows it to spring back after it strikes, making it perfect for the small repeated blows required in repoussage. Hold the hammer near the end of the shaft for maximum efficiency.

▼ Repoussé hammers are designed for making small, repeated blows.

► Pitch bowl supported on a basket base.

► Selection of commercial and custom chasing and doming punches.

WHAT'S THE PROBLEM?

SHAPING

DECORATION

WIREWORK

CASTING

STONE SETTING

Chasing a three-dimensional shape

1 Anneal, pickle and dry the piece of metal to be shaped. Either draw or scribe the pattern to be worked on to the metal.

2 Bend the four corners down at 90 degrees to form little spikes that will help to set the metal in the pitch. Play a bushy flame over the surface of the pitch to melt it, taking care not to let it bubble up too much, then set the piece into the pitch until the metal is sitting flush. Wet your fingers to prevent the pitch from sticking to them or use an old pair of tweezers to push the metal down.

3 Cool the whole bowl under a cold tap to firm up the pitch. The outline shape can now be chased with a lining tool, then depth added with blocking tools or doming punches. The metal will need to be removed from the pitch and annealed regularly as required.

4 Once the required depth is reached, remove the piece from the pitch. Gently heat any excess pitch on the metal until it turns to dust, or remove it with turpentine. Make sure all the pitch is removed before pickling the metal.

5 At this stage you can sharpen up the edge of the form and make it horizontal again with a planishing punch (a flat-faced tool).

6 Then bend the corners the opposite way and fill the hollow recess with melted pitch so that the piece is totally supported when you return it to the bowl of pitch.

7 You can now work on the front of the piece to introduce valleys and add detail as required. Once completed, use a lining tool to sharpen up the outer edge.

Soldering

Metals are usually joined with solder. This is an alloy that melts at a lower temperature than the metal, and results in an invisible, very strong bond. Different soldering alloys melt at different temperatures, allowing elaborate forms to be soldered without the whole piece collapsing.

▲ KATHARINA VONES
This intricately constructed ring uses multiple soldered joints.

The kind of soldering used in the construction of jewellery is referred to as hard soldering. When metal is heated its grain structure opens and the melted solder is drawn into these microscopic spaces, resulting in a new alloy comprising solder and the parent metal. Subsequent heating of the piece will help to reinforce this bond.

In general jewellers tend to work with a solder that is closest to the melting temperature of the metal being used; this results in the strongest and least detectable bond. Different solders are available for silver, and the various carats of gold. Copper solders are available in the US, but not so easy to source in Europe. Base metals can be soldered with silver solder, although this will result in a visible silvery solder line – the better your technique, the more invisible this line will be.

Successful soldering takes practice and nerve and will inevitably result in a couple of melted pieces to start with. This is best viewed as a rite of passage – mastering soldering techniques is very rewarding and can take designs in new and interesting directions.

▲▼ Strips of different grade solders

▲ Borax cone and dish

▶ Flux powder and liquid

Solder

Different grades of solder melt at different temperatures, and there are five grades available to jewellers (see table opposite). Different practitioners have their own views on which solder to use as a general purpose solder. If only one soldering joint is required, many prefer hard solder because it flows better than medium solder, whereas others insist that medium should be used because the metal does not need to be heated to such a high temperature, making firestain less likely. Both points are valid. The best option is to pick one and stick to it as your general purpose solder – you will get used to its behaviour, how it flows and the temperature at which it flows. Hard solder is the best colour match for silver as it contains the most silver.

Fluxes and antiflux

The word flux comes from the Latin *fluxus*, to flow, and is essential in getting the solder to go where you want it to. Without flux the melted solder balls up and remains static. Fluxes reduce the surface tension of the solder, allowing it to flow. Flux prevents oxides from forming on the joint, which would also inhibit solder flow.

Borax is the most generally used type of flux. It is available in powder or cone form. The powder form is simply mixed with water to make a thin paste. More commonly used is a borax cone and dish – the solid cone of borax is rubbed around the dish with a little water to make a thin paste that can be painted on to joints. Borax has a tendency to bubble up when heated, which can push the pallions of solder out of place; generally with even heating they return to their original placement.

Liquid flux (such as Auflux) This golden liquid flux is most frequently used for gold but can also be used for silver soldering. It does not bubble up and expand to the same extent as borax, but should be painted on several times as the metal is lightly heated to make sure that enough flux is introduced to the piece.

Tenacity 5 is best used for medium to high temperatures. It is useful when brazing stainless steel components, for example, because the steel's poor thermal conductivity means there is a risk of overheating, causing the flux to become exhausted and ineffective. The residue is hard to remove once it has been heated and has to be removed mechanically with emery.

Antiflux and heat insulators Various substances can be used to prevent solder from running on to a specific area (such as a hinge). Powdered polishing rouge mixed to a paste with water can be applied with a paintbrush. Similar pastes made with chalk or yellow ochre powder are also good. Graphite is also very effective and easy to apply accurately using a sharpened soft pencil.

To protect an existing soldered joint or a stone, a heat-insulating paste such as Thermogel or Technoflux can be used. Rouge powder made into a paste will also protect joints from heat up to a point. Remember not to quench any work with a stone in it, as the change in temperature can cause the stone to shatter.

◀ Heat insulators and rouge powder

Pickle

Once a piece has been soldered it will need to be pickled to remove oxides and residual flux (see page 41). It is worth mentioning here that one should take care to remove any steel binding wire before putting silver pieces into the pickle as this can result in copper being deposited on the surface of the silver (pickle plating). This has to be removed with emery paper, reheating and repickling.

SOLDER	MELTING TEMPERATURE	APPLICATIONS
Extra easy	690°C (1275°F)	Useful when making very large objects where it is difficult to hold the piece at a steady high temperature. Solder is in the form of wire and is best stick-fed into the prepared seam. It can also be used as the last solder in a particularly complex piece, or to solder a sprue into place when there is a risk of melting the other solder joints. It tends to be slightly yellowish in colour compared to the other silver solders.
Easy	715°C (1320°F)	For final solderings, and good for use on brooch backs or thin pieces of metal.
Medium	735°C (1355°F)	For use when you don't want to risk another soldering joint with hard solder.
Hard	750°C (1380°F)	General purpose soldering, flows well and produces strong joints. The first solder to be used in step soldering operations.
Enamelling	800°C (1470°F)	Very high melting point, which means that the piece will not fall apart in the kiln when being enamelled, nor will the solder run and interfere with the enamelling process. Remove flame as soon as the solder flows; the melting point of silver is close to this – 819°C (1506°F).
Soldering paste – all grades		A ready-mixed paste of solder and flux is available in syringe form. It is particularly useful for soldering small awkward pieces such as chain, but tends to result in weaker joints and is prone to spreading into areas where you might not want it. It is relatively expensive.

The solders above are available in silver, and also in the various colours and carats of gold. When soldering gold, always use the carat of the gold or a higher one.

WHAT'S THE PROBLEM?

SHAPING

DECORATION

WIREWORK

CASTING

STONE SETTING

Setting up a soldering station

Small soldering jobs can be conducted at the bench on a heatproof mat, but if you have the space available it is worth setting up a permanent soldering station in your workshop.

Make sure that the area is well ventilated and there is nothing flammable in the vicinity. It is a good idea to have a soldering station against a wall that can be protected with a heatproof mat. Ideally the area should be surrounded on three sides with heatproof bricks. The whole area should be cleaned regularly to make sure that no errant pieces of solder or flux can come in contact with work.

A selection of heatproof soldering blocks is essential, as are honeycomb ceramic soldering blocks with holes in them; these can be used with wires to hold the objects to be soldered. Charcoal blocks are very useful – when heated they reflect heat back on to the work, and they can hold wires and are easily modified with burrs or drills to accommodate the piece being soldered or to melt metal in. Steel meshes, or wigs, are very effective in that they allow the heat to reach the underside of an object, speeding up the soldering process. Strips of titanium folded into a V shape or zigzag are a useful alternative to a wig – they don't act as a heat sink.

A steel turntable can be handy to rotate work as it is being soldered. An anglepoise lamp is useful so that work can be set up under bright illumination, but when soldering commences it can be switched off to make it easier to observe the colour of the metal being heated more accurately.

Safety should be a primary consideration when setting up a soldering station. Position gas canisters on a flat surface out of the way where they cannot be knocked; they should be within easy reach and should always be switched off when not in use. It is a good idea to invest in a friction lighter, or buy a self-igniting handpiece such as those made by Rothenberger. Handpieces should be switched off when not in use.

A fire blanket and suitable fire extinguisher should be within easy reach, as should a first aid box and an eye wash kit. Cold running water is the best treatment for minor burns. If this is not available, keep a large bowl of cold water close by – it can also be used to quench work easily.

Torches

Most people start off with a small handheld chef's torch. These generally use lighter fuel and are just powerful enough to enable small pieces to be soldered and annealed. For small work a canister of MAPP or MAP-Pro gas and a pencil-flame torch is an excellent solution. It burns with quite a hot flame that might take some getting used to, but the tank size makes it much more useful than a handheld torch.

Propane and butane are easily available fuel sources and can be used with a regulator and torch head, such as the brazing torch used by plumbers that automatically mixes air with the gas. It is worthwhile fitting a finer burner tip than the brazing one that comes with the torch. This is the set-up used by most small workshops.

In colleges and large workshops a combination of the building's gas supply and pressurised air is used. This has the advantage of being more controllable because the flow of air can be regulated, but because of the highly flammable nature of oxygen it is not suitable for smaller workshops.

Micro-soldering systems produce oxygen and hydrogen from water. The flame they produce is intensely hot, so these are best suited for working on platinum and palladium or gold and silver chains. They are expensive and probably of limited use in a general jeweller's workshop.

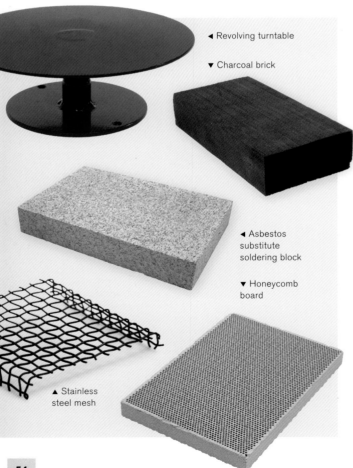

◄ Revolving turntable

▼ Charcoal brick

◄ Asbestos substitute soldering block

▼ Honeycomb board

▲ Stainless steel mesh

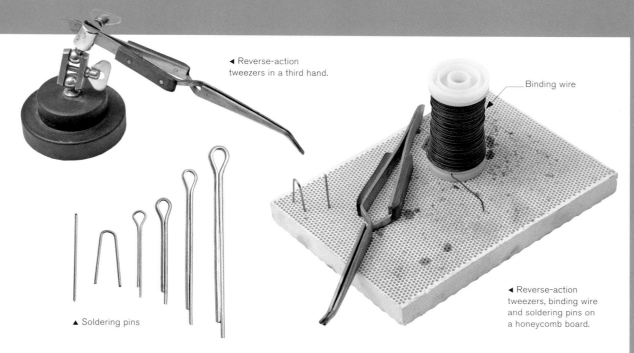

◄ Reverse-action tweezers in a third hand.

Binding wire

◄ Reverse-action tweezers, binding wire and soldering pins on a honeycomb board.

▲ Soldering pins

WHAT'S THE PROBLEM?

SHAPING

DECORATION

WIREWORK

CASTING

STONE SETTING

Supporting metals prior to soldering

It is well worth spending time setting up the hearth in the best way for each soldering job.

Reverse-action tweezers are extremely useful tools – use them to hold a piece of work upright or set them on top of firebricks to suspend a piece of work to be soldered to another. They can act as a heat sink, which can prevent the work from reaching the desired temperature for soldering, and can also get very hot and mark metal if overheated. They can be used in combination with a third hand, which is useful for holding work at a particular angle, or on a firebrick so that it does not move when another piece is introduced.

Binding wire is steel wire available in varying thicknesses. It is used to hold a piece of work together, or to attach one piece to another. Always make loops in binding wire as it is attached, to allow for expansion in the piece of work and to prevent the wire from marking the metal.

Soldering pins and clips (also known as cotter pins) are pins of various sizes made from steel wire; you can make the pins from binding wire as required for a particular job. Use binding wire or pins in conjunction with the small holes on honeycomb soldering blocks.

Solder trays and grain are useful for supporting small hard-to-hold pieces. Silicon carbide grains are completely inert and work can be semi-submerged in them.

THE FIVE RULES OF SOLDERING

1	Metal should be clean – dirt, grease, oxides, graphite or carbon can all inhibit solder flow. Generally, heating and pickling are adequate to remove these. Make sure that any pickle is rinsed off the object before heating.
2	Joint should be tight – solder does not bridge gaps, so the distance between parts should be minimal; you should not be able to see light through them. They should be well finished and free from burrs that might prevent good contact.
3	Solder flows towards the heat – try to get both sides of the object being soldered to reach the same temperature at the same time. If one side is hotter than the other, the solder will head to that side and will not join properly.
4	Don't use too much solder – it adds lots of time to the cleaning up process. Economic use of solder means that you will not have to attack the work with abrasives to get it off.
5	Be brief – it is good practice to make the soldering operation as efficient as possible. Prolonged heating can spend the flux and oxidise the metal. Move the torch around the work with purpose, using the hottest part of the flame.

Soldering methods

There are various methods for applying solder to work – practising them all will mean that the best method for the job is available to you.

Pallion soldering This is generally the first method to be taught in jewellery classes. Cut small squares of solder (pallions) with tin snips. Dip them in flux and place on the fluxed joint. Bring the torch towards the piece slowly to

prevent the pallions from being blown away. Heat the metal evenly on each side of the joint until they reach the temperature at which the solder melts. Remove the flame as soon as the solder runs.

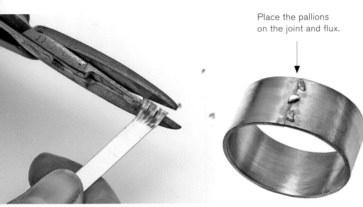

Place the pallions on the joint and flux.

▲ Cut pallions of solder with tin snips.

▲ Heat both sides of the joint evenly.

Sweat soldering This is used to solder one piece of metal on top of another. Make sure that both surfaces are clean. Place the pieces together in their final position and draw around the edge of the smaller piece with a soft pencil, then shade heavily the area that needs to be protected from solder (or use rouge powder and water to mark the area).

Gently heat and then apply flux to the reverse side of the piece that will be on top (the smaller piece). Arrange pallions of solder on the surface and heat until they melt. Pickle and rinse this piece. Flux the areas to be soldered on both

pieces, making sure that the flux does not extend as far as the pencilled exclusion zone. Put both pieces together and apply even heat all over until the solder melts. This can be hard to gauge as you cannot see it, but it can usually be felt if you apply very slight pressure to the top piece with a soldering pick. Sometimes a very fine line of solder becomes visible around the edge as it flows. Sometimes you just have to make an educated guess based on the colour of the metal and the length of time it has been heated for. If the piece comes apart when quenched, start again.

Use a pencil to shade in the area to be protected from solder.

▲ Heat to melt the pallions of solder.

▲ Use a soldering pick to gauge when the solder has melted between the pieces.

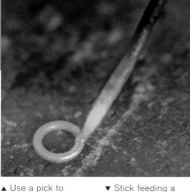

Using a soldering pick This is a useful skill to acquire and can be used when it might be problematic to place a pallion of solder on the work, such as in chain making. Arrange a selection of pallions on a firebrick or charcoal block (they are easier to see against the black charcoal). Prepare the joint and lightly heat it, then direct the flame at the end of the probe as you pick up a pallion of solder. The pallion should ball up and adhere to the end of the pick. Heat the work to be soldered. As it reaches the right temperature, introduce the small piece of solder on the end of the pick – it should flow straight into the joint. Getting the temperature right for this does take a bit of practice, but it is worth it.

▲ Use a pick to transfer solder to the heated joint.

▼ Stick feeding a joint with solder.

Stick feeding This method is useful when soldering a long or very large piece of metal. Like using a pick it takes practice. Prepare the joint to be soldered. Cut a long thin stick of solder and hold it with reverse-action tweezers. Heat the metal to be soldered until it reaches soldering temperature. Follow behind the torch as it moves along the metal, holding the stick of solder and dragging it along the joint. As the torch moves along it pulls the solder in the right direction. Take care not to heat the solder directly because it will melt, leaving unsightly blobs on the joint.

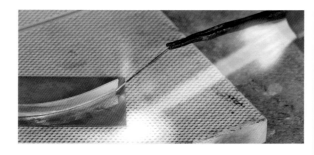

Other joining methods

Fusing It is possible to join two pieces of silver without using solder at all by fluxing them and taking them up to melting temperature, which welds the two pieces together. Clean and flux both pieces, then heat evenly until very close to melting point (when dark patches start to appear on the surface). Play the flame around so that all parts of the metal reach this state. Pull the flame away at the first sign of reticulation (melting).

Apply flux prior to fusing.

▲ Heat until very close to melting point.

Laser welding Laser welding units have very good microscopes and can achieve extremely fine invisible joints. As with PUK welding, laser welding is best achieved on gold and platinum because silver and base metals tend to spatter. For this reason it is also useful for tacking work together before normal soldering. Because they are so expensive, getting a chance to use one may be problematic.

Pulse arc welding Micro-versions of a TIG (tungsten inert gas) welder, such as the PUK welder, have been especially developed for the jewellery industry. They work by forming an arc between a tungsten electrode and the piece for joining. This is performed in an inert gas atmosphere. The length and strength of the welding pulse can be altered depending on the material being welded. It is very useful for joining jump rings. The joints are not as strong as hard-soldered pieces, but it is useful for tacking a particularly complex piece prior to conventional soldering.

▼ PUK pulse arc welder

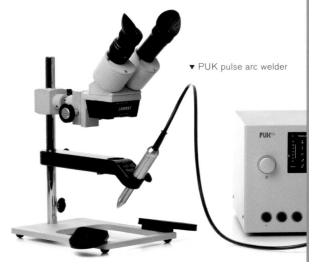

WHAT'S THE PROBLEM?

SHAPING

DECORATION

WIREWORK

CASTING

STONE SETTING

Riveting

Unsoldered joining methods are known as cold connections. Rivets are pieces of rod, wire or tube that fit tightly into drilled holes. Their ends are then punched, or upset, to lock the pieces together.

Rivets are hugely versatile. As well as holding two materials tightly together, they can hold materials at a specific distance apart using spacers. They can also be used as pivots, allowing one area to swing away from another. If you want to fix two pieces securely and rigidly, it is best to use two or more rivets.

▲ MARIANNE ANDERSON
These brooches use functional rivets that double as decorative elements.

CROSS-SECTIONS OF COMMONLY USED RIVETS

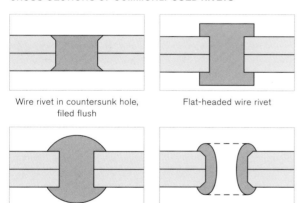

Wire rivet in countersunk hole, filed flush

Flat-headed wire rivet

Domed wire rivet

Tube rivet in countersunk hole

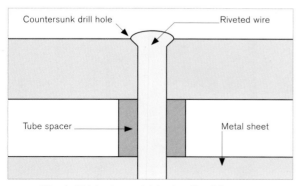

Countersunk drill hole

Riveted wire

Tube spacer

Metal sheet

Wire rivet joining two metal sheets, with a tube spacer

Making a basic rivet

The simplest form of rivet is made from a piece of wire that should be of exactly the same diameter as the hole it will fit into. Anneal the wire and place it in the protected jaws of a vice. Tap it gently with a ball-peen hammer, starting in the centre and radiating the taps around the top of the rivet outwards in a spiral to create a nail head.

Insert the rivet through the holes in the piece of work. Cut the protruding wire close to the workpiece with end cutters. File the end of the wire flat – it should protrude no more than 1mm from the piece or it will bend when being hammered. Hammer this protruding end gently with a riveting hammer to form the rivet head.

▲ Hammer the wire rivet to form the nail head.

▲ Insert the rivet into the hole in the work.

Making tube rivets

Cut a section of tube in a chenier vice, 2mm longer than the combined length of the pieces being joined. Drill holes of the same width as the tubing and countersink on both sides to allow the tube to be spread. Anneal and pickle the tube and insert into the hole. Use a scribe or burnisher and a hammer to open up one end of the tube slightly, then turn over and repeat. Once the ends are spread enough, use a doming punch or ball-peen hammer to flatten them further.

▲ Cut sections of tube to use as rivets.

Making countersunk rivets

Drill holes in the workpiece to accept the rivets, then use a round burr slightly larger than the drill bit to create a countersink on the surface of the material. Make rivets in the usual way, making sure that the upset area is large enough to fill the countersink hole. Insert each rivet, hammer the protruding ends into the countersink holes and then file back until the rivet is flush with the surface. On metals of the same colour, the rivets will be invisible.

▲ Use a round burr to create countersink holes.

▲ Hammer and then file the rivets flush with the workpiece.

Using a headpin as a rivet

It is possible to ball up one end of a piece of silver wire using heat to make a headpin that can be used as a rivet. Flux the end of a piece of wire, holding it pointing downwards in front of some firebricks. Heat the end with the hottest part of the flame; the metal will melt and ball up.

If the ball gets too large, it will fall off. These ball-shaped rivets can be used as a decorative feature on a riveted piece. The wire can be fitted into a corresponding hole in a draw plate and flattened with a planishing hammer to give it a flat head if required.

◄ Heat the end of a piece of wire to make a headpin rivet.

Using a rivet sleeve as a spacer

Tubing can be used between elements to create space between them. Select tube that fits the rivet wire neatly – if the tube is too wide, the wire will have room to bend. Make a rivet head on one end of the wire, then thread the rivet through the assembled parts using the tube as a spacer between them. Upset the rivet on the top layer and finish the rivet heads as required. It is possible to use this technique with two pieces of tube that fit one inside the other.

▲ Tubing used as rivet sleeves to create space between pieces of work.

WHAT'S THE PROBLEM?

SHAPING

DECORATION

WIREWORK

CASTING

STONE SETTING

Hinges

Hinges join and allow articulation between two elements in a piece of jewellery. They are most commonly used in lockets and bangles. Before constructing a piece of articulated jewellery, it is worth doing some hinge research – from biscuit tins to piano lids, and of course doors, hinges are everywhere.

◄ **TIFFANY BAEHLER**
The cubes of this bracelet are articulated with concealed hinges.

▲ **ALEX MONROE**
A steel spring can be used as a central knuckle on a piece. Whether the piece springs open or closed depends on which side of the object the ends of the spring are trapped.

Hinges can be concealed or visible; they can move freely or stop when at 180 degrees. A simple hinge can be made from tabs of metal that extend from a piece and wrap around a bar, or just a rivet inserted in a hole drilled through two notched pieces of metal. The most commonly used hinges in a jewellery context are three- or five-knuckled hinges made from tube. The middle section is soldered on to one half of the piece and the end sections on to the other half, then riveted together with a hinge pin.

Hinges should be the last piece of construction undertaken prior to polishing. The construction of a hinge calls for a degree of accuracy and patience – the soldering part can be tricky.

Knotched joint

1 Make sure the two halves of the knotched element fit together neatly.

2 Tape the pieces together to align them. Drill a hole through both pieces; use a bench drill and a drill press clamp for accuracy.

3 If an invisible hinge pin is required, make pilot holes at each end. Lubricate and insert the hinge pin.

4 Rivet the ends of the pin. Continue adding elements to the construction as required.

◄ This simple hinge mechanism is often used in bracelets where repeated forms are riveted together, such as this acrylic bangle.

WHAT'S THE PROBLEM?

SHAPING

DECORATION

WIREWORK

CASTING

STONE SETTING

Three-knuckled hinge

In this hinge, two outer knuckles are soldered to one half of the construction, the centre knuckle to the other and a hinge pin slots through them.

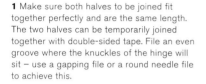

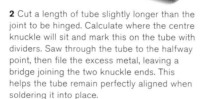

1 Make sure both halves to be joined fit together perfectly and are the same length. The two halves can be temporarily joined together with double-sided tape. File an even groove where the knuckles of the hinge will sit – use a gapping file or a round needle file to achieve this.

2 Cut a length of tube slightly longer than the joint to be hinged. Calculate where the centre knuckle will sit and mark this on the tube with dividers. Saw through the tube to the halfway point, then file the excess metal, leaving a bridge joining the two knuckle ends. This helps the tube remain perfectly aligned when soldering it into place.

3 Paint antiflux on any areas that should not get soldered, including the ends of the knuckles. Flux carefully the areas that should be soldered. Allow the whole construction to dry completely before proceeding. Use binding wire to secure the knuckles in place, adding tension loops where necessary.

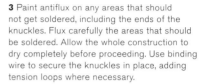

4 Solder the tubing to the piece, using as little solder as possible. When the binding wire is removed, one half of the construction should release. The central bridge can then be sawn off and filed neatly.

5 Cut tubing for the central knuckle and make sure that it sits tightly next to the outer ones. Solder it into place. An oiled piece of steel or old drill bit makes a good temporary hinge pin to ensure correct alignment.

6 The hinge pin that holds the construction together should be a very tight fit. Put a length longer than the hinge in a pin vice and file a point on it.

7 Lubricate the pin with a little candlewax or beeswax and twist it into the tube knuckles of the hinge.

8 Cut the ends off the hinge pin, file flat and then rivet the ends to make them secure. Silver hinge pins loosen with use, so it is best if they are quite tight to start with.

▲ The finished hinged piece.

Cutting and piercing

THE PROBLEM

Impossible to saw in a straight line

Sawing in a straight line takes practice and initially the saw blade seems to have a life of its own. Constantly observe and correct the line.

Caused by: The sawblade is not tight enough or is upside down.

THE SOLUTIONS

Make sure the saw blade is the correct way up: With the handle towards you, when you stroke the blade from the handle to the end of the saw it should feel rough.
Tighten the saw blade: Secure the handle of the blade tightly, then push the edge of the saw frame just below the nut against the bench peg and simultaneously tighten it.

Fasten the bench peg securely: This will prevent it from moving up and down as you saw.
Hold the handle of the saw gently: Try not to tense up.

▲ Saw line is not straight and is drifting away from the guideline.

▲ Check that teeth are facing upwards and towards the saw handle.

▲ Press the saw frame against the bench and tighten the saw blade so that it is taut.

▲ It should ping when plucked.

▲ Start by running the saw blade from the top end to the handle end to make a notch. Use your thumbnail as a guide.

▲ Keep the sawing hand relaxed and use the whole length of the saw.

▲ Hold the metal firmly in your non-sawing hand and keep fingers away from the blade.

THE PROBLEM

Can't see what I'm meant to be cutting

Problems can be compounded if it is hard to see what needs to be cut. A clearly drawn line can make life much easier.

Caused by: A poorly lit working environment; the transcribed design or image is hard to read on the metal.

THE SOLUTIONS

Make sure your bench area is well lit: Make sure that there is as much natural light as possible. Augment this with an anglepoise lamp fitted with a bright bulb – preferably a daylight one. This can be tilted to catch the light on a scribed line.

Ensure your design is easy to read: Printed or photocopied designs attached to metal with double-sided tape work best. If using a pen, make sure it is a fine-tipped permanent pen so that the drawing does not get rubbed off before sawing is finished.

Stick a printed design on to the metal with double-sided tape.

Thinly drawn lines are easier to follow with the saw blade.

▲ If it is hard to see the design on the metal, it will be impossible to cut with any accuracy.

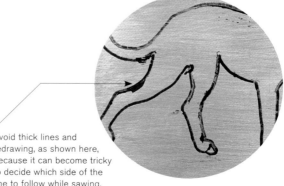

Avoid thick lines and redrawing, as shown here, because it can become tricky to decide which side of the line to follow while sawing.

THE PROBLEM

Saw blade keeps breaking

Even the most experienced jeweller breaks saw blades. Always buy the best you can afford, because not all saw blades are created equal.

Caused by: Using the wrong size of saw blade; not holding the metal firmly enough; incorrect handling of the blade; too much pressure on the blade; using only a small part of the blade when sawing.

THE SOLUTIONS

Use the correct size of blade:
Two or three teeth on the saw blade should fit against the metal width (see page 36).
Hold metal firmly: Use your left hand (or non-sawing hand) to hold the piece of metal firmly on the bench peg, otherwise it can jump up, twisting the blade and making it snap.
Handle the blade correctly:
■ Don't push too hard on the blade – saw gently, let the blade do the work and don't rush.
■ Hold the handle of the saw gently.
■ Don't go around corners too quickly or the blade will twist and break.
■ Keep the saw blade moving up and down constantly, and pull back slightly while moving the saw up and down to create some space when going around corners.
■ Use the whole length of the blade because concentrating on a short area will wear it out.
■ Once you have finished piercing, loosen the saw blade because keeping it under tension for a long time will weaken it.

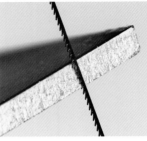

▲ Check that two or three teeth fit against the metal width.

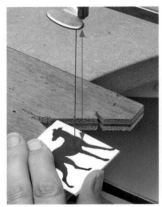

▲ Use the whole length of the saw blade to prevent wear on one area of the blade.

THE PROBLEM

Saw blade keeps getting stuck in the metal

This is a problem that tends to disappear with practice. Often in an effort to free the blade it can get twisted and break.

Caused by: Pushing too hard with the saw blade; the blade twisting as you move.

THE SOLUTIONS

Lubricate the blade: For ease of movement, run a piece of beeswax or an ordinary household candle down the back of the blade. If you don't have a candle, saliva will also work.
If the blade is twisting as you cut:
Release your hold on the metal and let the blade return to its natural position before you resume sawing gently.

▲ Try not to get wax in the teeth of the saw, as this traps metal dust and makes it hard to see where the saw is cutting.

fix-its　Filing

THE PROBLEM

Filing seems to be making more marks than there were before

Filing should only be carried out where necessary — to remove solder, to remove casting lines or to eradicate the marks generated by sawing. Try to keep protective film or masking tape on metal for as long as possible during the making process to minimise scratches. Filing should be followed by abrading with emery paper.

Caused by: File is too rough; file may be full of large particles of metal that are leaving marks; file is too small for the job.

THE SOLUTIONS

Wrap the file with emery paper: If you don't have any fine files, try wrapping some emery paper around your file.

Clean the file: Use a file brush to clean the file or a small piece of copper, running the edge of it methodically across the file in the cut grooves. As you do this, the copper will be filed into the shape of the grooves and will take out any foreign material. Rubbing chalk into the file after cleaning should prevent this from happening again too soon.

Use the right size file: Use the biggest file you can for a job, so that you can cover the largest area all at once. Using a needle file when you should be using a hand file can make a straight line look like castle battlements.

Keep your wrist flexible when filing curves: When filing the shank of a ring, or any curved object, make sure that your wrist is flexible and follows the profile of the curve being filed — keeping your wrist rigid will result in a profile like a hexagon or worse.

Files can be cleaned with a scrap of copper.

THE PROBLEM

File does not seem to be working or can't reach into all areas

Caused by: Work is not properly supported, making filing inefficient; file might be skidding as it is full of particles of metal; the file may be too big for the job.

THE SOLUTIONS

Support your work: Make sure your work is supported on a bench peg as this will help the forward stroke of the file be more efficient.

Clean the file: Clean as above using a piece of copper.

Use alternative tools for fine work: The smallest files available are escapement files, but even these might be too thick. If this is the case, roll a piece of emery paper around a length of wire, or just around itself. Or fold a small strip of emery in half and hold it between your fingers on each side of the piece and move it back and forth. A strip can also be fastened in a vice and held taut while the work is moved on it. Abrasive tape and cord in various widths and grades are available from jewellery suppliers for fine work.

◀ Use emery paper held in a vice to get into small pierced areas.

THE PROBLEM

Metal has melted

With practice you will notice the warning signs that a piece might be on the verge of melting — silver goes slightly grey, and shimmering spots start to appear just prior to the whole thing liquefying.

Caused by: Forge area may be too brightly lit — it is easier to see what colour the metal is in dim light (the annealing temperature for silver gives a pale orange colour).

◄ When metal is over-annealed, it will begin to melt.

THE SOLUTIONS

Rescue or recycle: This might not be the end of the world.
- If you have caught it in time, it may be possible to file back the distortions.
- At the end of the project you might be able to flood the 'valleys' with solder.
- If you are lucky, you can make a feature of it — reticulation can look great.
- Even if you have to bite the bullet and admit that the piece is dead, the metal can be recycled.

▲ You may be able to file back the distortions for a satisfactory result.

▲ Place pallions of solder on to the affected area.

▲ Heat the area to flood the depressions with solder, then sand back.

THE PROBLEM

Metal is stiff and hard to work

Caused by: It has been under-annealed, which can happen when metal is quite thick.

THE SOLUTIONS

Re-anneal the metal: Re-anneal it and hold it at annealing temperature for longer — up to 10 seconds.

Hold and move the torch correctly: Make sure that the torch is being held at the correct distance from the metal. Move the torch slowly along the metal.

▲ Torch at correct distance from metal.

WHAT'S THE PROBLEM?

SHAPING

DECORATION

WIREWORK

CASTING

STONE SETTING

THE PROBLEM

A grey shadow has appeared on sterling silver

This is known as firestain. There are several ways of fixing this — most of them involve elbow grease.

Caused by: The copper in the alloy oxidising. Pickling usually removes firescale on the surface of the silver, but often the deeper firestain is only revealed at the polishing stage. Firestain on a piece can easily be revealed by placing a piece of tracing paper over it.

Firestain often becomes visible after polishing.

▲ Tracing paper can be useful to easily see how much firestain is left when removing it.

THE SOLUTIONS

Buff the piece: Use a water of Ayr stone or fine emery paper on a buff stick or wrapped around a suitable file. Alternatively, buff with a short bristle mop on a polishing motor (it will get hot!). Sometimes reverting to the tripoli stage of polishing and being very thorough is sufficient to remove firestain.

Bright dipping: Once the piece is constructed, attach a wire to it and dip for a few seconds in a warm 50:50 solution of nitric acid and water. This is a technique used by enamellers to remove firestain. Obviously this must be performed with extreme caution – always add acid to water, and wear protective clothing and goggles.

Use argentium silver: Argentium silver has a small amount of germanium in place of some of the copper in the alloy and this prevents firestain. This alloy behaves slightly differently from sterling silver so should be researched prior to use.

Reduce the amount of oxygen: It can be prevented by heating in an oxygen-free environment but this is very hard to achieve. The amount of oxygen reaching the surface can be reduced by coating the metal with a non-oxidising powder such as borax and methylated spirits or water, or a product such as Argotect. The piece must then be well pickled to ensure the removal of all the flux, which can damage tools.

▲ Use a water of Ayr stone to remove firestain by abrasive means.

▲ Alternatively, use a buff stick to remove firestain.

▲ Bright dip the piece in a solution of nitric acid and water.

The firestain has disappeared from the area dipped in acid.

THE PROBLEM

Edges to be soldered have a gap between them

Although a straight line was cut through both sides of the ring, when put together a V-shaped gap has appeared.

Caused by: The strip of metal that forms the ring was not absolutely parallel when bent up.

THE SOLUTION

Use the saw blade as a tiny file: It is best to address this problem – although it would be possible to make the two ends of the ring fit together, this would result in the ring being a slightly conical shape. Hold the ring on the end of the saw peg, with the open part of the V shape facing upwards, and saw down through the gap from top to bottom. Repeat this until the edges meet perfectly.

▲ Use a saw blade to 'file' the edges straight.

◀ V-shaped gap where edges should meet perfectly.

THE PROBLEM

Edges to be soldered don't meet at all

Caused by: The ring has become work-hardened and springy. If the shank is quite wide or thick, manipulating it can be a struggle.

THE SOLUTIONS

Use ring pliers to bring the ends together: Re-anneal the ring and use ring pliers to get the ends to meet. Push one end underneath the other, then turn over and repeat with the other side. This should create enough tension so that the ends meet nicely.

Use binding wire to hold edges together: Binding wire can be used to hold the edges together when soldering. Remember to put a loop in the wire to allow for expansion.

◀ The metal is too hard to bring the ends together.

▲ Use ring pliers to overlap the edges slightly.

▲ You should then be able to bring the edges neatly together.

THE PROBLEM

Ring isn't round

Caused by:
When bending and manipulating the ring, it has gone out of shape.

THE SOLUTION

Refine the shape on a mandrel: Prior to soldering it does not mattr if the ring is not round. After soldering, it can be trued up on a mandrel using a soft mallet.

◄ The ring has become misshapen during forming.

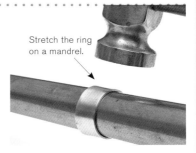

▲ Use a mallet and mandrel to create a perfect round shape.

THE PROBLEM

Ring is too small or too large

Remember that it is easier to make a small ring slightly larger than a large ring smaller.

Caused by: Sometimes measurements go wrong; fingers change size depending on the temperature; ring stick sizes can vary slightly.

THE SOLUTIONS

Enlarge on a mandrel: If the ring is too small, anneal it and place it on a mandrel. Tap lightly with a hammer, regularly moving the ring around the mandrel so that the metal is stretched evenly. Check the size regularly.

Cut out a piece to reduce size: If the ring is too large, cut a small piece out on either side of the soldered joint. Check the size and make any adjustments before re-soldering.

▶ Remove 1.3mm to reduce by one ring size.

Stretch the ring on a mandrel.

THE PROBLEM

Marks on the ring

Caused by: This may be because the wrong type of pliers have been used, or ring pliers have been used back to front – always make sure the curved side of the pliers is used on the inside of the ring and the flat face on the outside.

THE SOLUTION

Use hammer, file and emery paper: Hammer the ring on a mandrel with a soft mallet to remove any large ridges. File until the gouges disappear and then use various grades of emery paper until the metal is smooth.

▲ Using ring pliers the wrong way around will leave marks.

▲ The correct way – keep the curved leg on the inner curve.

THE PROBLEM

Metal cracks and fractures

Occasionally when forging a split can appear in the metal.

Caused by: It has been under-annealed in relation to how much it has been worked and the metal has become fatigued. Over-annealing at too high a temperature or for too long can also result in cracking due to the structure of the metal changing and becoming coarse.

THE SOLUTIONS

Remove the affected metal: Saw off the affected part, re-anneal and continue.

Patch up the holes: If you are near the end of the project, try patching up holes with wire or shims of silver, and then solder. File or sand back.

Adjust technique: Keep hammer blows in one direction at a time between annealings to minimise stress on the metal.

Use the correct cooling method: Various metals should be cooled in different ways after annealing. For example, red gold alloys should be quenched promptly in cold water; allowing them to air cool makes them brittle. Conversely, brass should be air cooled rather than quenched in cold water. (See table of cooling methods on page 40.)

▲ Saw off the affected area and continue.

▲ Alternatively, patch up the cracks with shims of silver solder.

▲ After soldering, file and sand back the patched areas.

THE PROBLEM

Metal is bending

Caused by: Hammer strokes are weighted more on one side of the piece than the other, or hammer is not being held properly.

▲ Bent rod

THE SOLUTIONS

Hammer back into shape: Pause and examine the piece – one edge will be wider than the other. Concentrate your hammer blows on the wider side; the curve should even up.

Adjust the angle of hammering: Make sure that the hammer is striking the metal straight on. It might be necessary to adjust the angle at which the hammer is held, or change the height of the work.

▼ Concentrate hammer blows on the wider side.

▼ The metal should eventually straighten out.

▶ Hold the hammer near the end of the handle.

WHAT'S THE PROBLEM?

SHAPING

DECORATION

WIREWORK

CASTING

STONE SETTING

THE PROBLEM

Unwanted marks appearing on metal

Caused by: Marks on the face of the hammer (one mark on the hammer will result in a thousand marks on the work); the hammer not hitting the work properly and making a dent; the type of hammer being used.

THE SOLUTIONS

File and sand to remove marks: Stop working as soon as you notice this happening and file and sand as necessary to remove marks.

Check the hammer face: A nick in a raising hammer can be removed with emery paper. Put the hammer in a vice and use a length of abrasive tape in a manner similar to shining shoes. Work up through the grades, then finish by polishing the face of the hammer on a polishing motor.

Adjust your hammering angle: Make sure that the face of the hammer is hitting the work properly or it can make dents. This can happen if the piece is too high, such as on top of a stake held in a vice at bench height – in this instance, find something stable to stand on.

Smooth out ridges with a planishing hammer: If the piece has been stretched with a cross-peen hammer, this will create ridged hammer marks. These need to be flattened down with a planishing hammer, taking care that they don't fold over on themselves and crack.

Nicks on the hammer face.

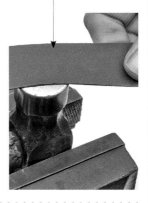

Use emery paper to smooth out the nicks.

THE PROBLEM

Brass rod keeps fracturing when being worked

Caused by: There are are two manufacturing processes for rod – drawing and extruding. Extruded rod is more brittle and prone to cracking.

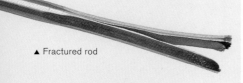

▲ Fractured rod

THE SOLUTIONS

Saw off the end: Saw off the affected part, re-anneal the metal and then continue to work very gently – fracturing may reoccur.

Use drawn rod: Check with the supplier and always favour drawn rod.

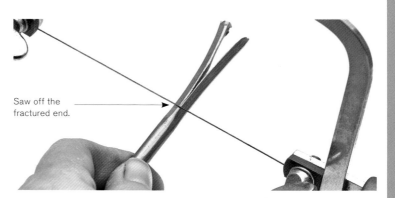

Saw off the fractured end.

THE PROBLEM

Rod is tapering, but the end is turning into a tube

Caused by: This tends to happen as the metal is displaced.

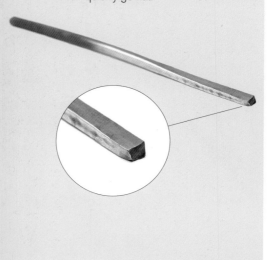

THE SOLUTION

Saw or file off the end: Keep an eye on it and occasionally saw or file off the end when this happens, then keep hammering or use a file for the final taper point.

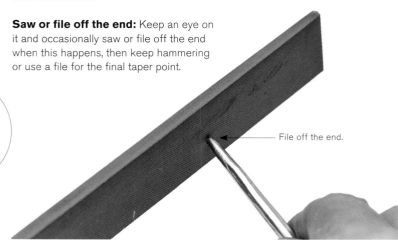

File off the end.

THE PROBLEM

Rod isn't tapering; it's just going flat

Caused by: It is important to keep the piece square in section at the end or it will tend to turn into a rhombus shape. If you don't pay attention at that point, it can quickly go flat.

THE SOLUTION

Pay attention and act fast: As soon as you catch it becoming rhombus shaped, pay attention to your hammer strokes to restore it to the square shape. Once it has become flattened, it is unlikely that you will be able to retrieve it.

Hammer back into a square shape as soon as you notice the problem developing.

WHAT'S THE PROBLEM?

SHAPING

DECORATION

WIREWORK

CASTING

STONE SETTING

fix-its

Doming and swaging

THE PROBLEM

Domed piece has marks or ridges on the underside

Caused by: The piece of metal has been forced into a hollow that is too small for it and the lip has marked the metal.

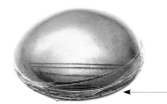

Ridges on the underside of the metal.

▲ The hollow is too small for the metal.

THE SOLUTIONS

Use the correct size hollow: Always make sure that the metal fits comfortably into the hollow in the block – start with a large one and work down to the size you want. If the disc of metal is too large to fit in your doming block, it can be started on a sandbag or a depression in a tree stump.

Clean out the hollow: Always check that there is no dirt or grit on the doming hollow before putting the metal into it.

File back the marks: It may be possible to remove the marks with a file if they are not too deep.

THE PROBLEM

Domed piece has marks and ridges on the inside

Caused by: The doming punch has marks on it. This is caused when a punch is forced into a doming hollow that is too small for it, and the punch will now mark any metal it comes in contact with.

Ridges on the inside of the metal.

Marks on the doming punch.

THE SOLUTION

Sand out the marks from the punch: Place the punch upright in a vice and use emery paper to sand out the marks. Use a strip of emery and move it as if shining shoes. Work up through the grades, then finish by polishing the face of the doming punch.

▲ Using the wrong size punch for the hollow will cause the punch to become marked.

▼ Hold the punch in a vice and sand off the marks with emery paper.

THE PROBLEM

Domed piece has uneven indentations on it

Caused by:
Using too small a punch.

▶ The punch is too small.

THE SOLUTION

Use the right size punch: Always make sure that the punch you use is the right size. It should fit entirely inside the hollow, leaving enough room for the thickness of metal. Anneal the dome and use a larger punch on it. As you move down the sizes of hollow in the doming block, always match the doming punch to the indentation.

▲ Indentations on the metal.

THE PROBLEM

Edges of swaged piece don't meet neatly

Caused by: Sometimes the edge can become uneven as metal is stretched.

THE SOLUTION

Hammer and then saw the edges: Anneal the piece and hammer on a metal rod until contact is made between the edges. Run a piercing saw down the seam to remove any protrusions. Repeat until the seam is perfect.

▲ Hammer until edges meet.

▲ Run a saw blade down the seam to neaten.

THE PROBLEM

Narrow but thick-walled tube is required – it is very hard to bend up

Caused by: It is very hard to bend up narrow lengths of metal if they are more than 24 gauge (0.5mm).

THE SOLUTIONS

Use a draw plate: Start with a much wider piece of metal of the required thickness. Make up into a tube, adding a V shape at the end. Pull it through a draw plate until it achieves the correct diameter, remembering to anneal regularly.
Use a vice: If you don't have a swage block, the strip of metal can be placed in the slightly open jaws of a vice.

▼ You can use a vice as an alternative to a swage block.

WHAT'S THE PROBLEM?

SHAPING

DECORATION

WIREWORK

CASTING

STONE SETTING

fix-its
Repoussage and chasing

THE PROBLEM

A split has appeared on the piece being repousséd

Always stop as soon as you notice this happening — it will only get worse.

Caused by: The punch or chasing tool being used might have rough or sharp edges; metal might be too thin; metal may have been under-annealed for the amount it has been stretched.

THE SOLUTIONS

Smooth out your tools: Use emery paper to remove any sharp areas off the tools you are using and then repolish.

Fill the split: Remove the piece from the pitch and clean. From the back, flood the area to be repaired with hard solder. It may be necessary to cut a shim of metal to fill any gaps — solder in place with hard solder. File and emery until the repair is invisible. From now on, any further annealing and repoussage should be carried out cautiously.

▲ Insert a shim of metal into the fissure, with a pallion of solder next to it.

▲ File back the shim after it has been soldered in place.

THE PROBLEM

Pitch has become brittle and bubbly

Caused by: It has been overheated.

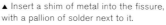

THE SOLUTIONS

Skim off the surface: Have some old newspaper on hand — gently heat the pitch and skim off the top layer with a piece of scrap metal or an old spoon on to the paper.

Use minimal heat: Try to use a minimum amount of heat to warm the pitch in the future.

◀ Overheated pitch

THE PROBLEM

Form has collapsed

Caused by: The metal was not properly supported by the pitch, or the pitch may have had a bubble in it.

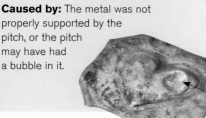

Collapsed form

THE SOLUTION

Punch out the collapsed area: Remove from the pitch and clean the piece. Replace the opposite way up in the pitch and punch out the collapsed area. Remove, clean and anneal, then pour molten pitch into the recessed area until it is flush. Allow to cool. Replace in the pitch and continue.

▲ Punch out the collapsed area from the other side, then continue.

THE PROBLEM

The joint hasn't soldered

THE CAUSES

Hasn't soldered at all: Sometimes the draft caused by the torch flame is enough to blow the solder away. If you have used quite a lot of flux and it is bubbling up, you can miss this fact.

Solder hasn't run: Not enough heat has been applied to allow the solder to run. Or the heat was not intense enough, but was held on the piece for so long that the flux has burned away, resulting in the solder not flowing.

Solder has balled up but hasn't run: Too much heat was applied to the solder joint rather than over the whole piece, or sufficient heat did not reach the joint (opposite factors sometimes have the same result). Either the flux has become exhausted or there is dirt or grease on the piece, preventing the solder from running.

▲ Not soldered at all.

▲ Solder hasn't run.

▲ Solder has balled up but hasn't run.

THE SOLUTIONS

Try again: Pickle, rinse, reflux and re-solder, paying close attention when you introduce the torch to the piece – keep a close eye on the pallions!

Adjust the heat: Pickle, rinse, reflux and try again, using a large bushy flame to get the whole area around the joint to heat up quickly and efficiently.

Clean up and try again: Remove the balls of solder, pickle and rinse the piece. Reflux, using a fine paintbrush to apply the flux so that it only goes where it is needed. Add some small pallions of solder to make sure there is enough to flow into the joint, and re-solder.

▲ Make sure the metal is scrupulously clean before soldering.

▲ Flux the joint, dip the pallions in flux and then place them on the joint.

▲ Pickle the piece after soldering to remove residual flux and oxides.

WHAT'S THE PROBLEM?

SHAPING

DECORATION

WIREWORK

CASTING

STONE SETTING

THE PROBLEM

Solder has run but the joint isn't successful

THE CAUSES

Only part of the joint has soldered:
The joint has a gap in it – solder will not bridge a gap; the joint needs to fit perfectly. The piece or your hands are not clean – solder will not flow over grease or polishing compounds.

Solder has stayed on one side of joint: Too much heat was applied to one side of the joint; edges of the joint are not close enough.

Joint looked alright but has broken:
This sometimes happens once you put a ring on the mandrel to true it up. Solder will flow where the flux is – this might be due to not enough solder or too widely spread flux. The piece may have been overheated, causing the solder to be absorbed into the metal. It might be due to contaminants on the seam.

THE SOLUTIONS

▲ Only one part of joint has soldered.

▲ Solder has stayed on one side of joint.

▲ Broken joint.

Adjust the fit of the joint: Saw open the part that has soldered and make sure that the joint is light tight (see below).
Clean everything scrupulously:
Make sure that the piece is completely clean, particularly of grease or polishing compounds. Also make sure that your hands are clean and grease-free.

Concentrate the heat where needed:
Pickle, rinse, reflux and concentrate heat more on the opposite side. Sometimes you can use the torch heat to pull the solder where you need it.
Make the joint light-tight: Check that the joint is light-tight; if not, run a saw blade down through the gap, repeating as necessary to get a good, tight fit.

Clean up and try again: Run a sheet of emery between the joint to remove any contaminants, then scrub with liquid detergent on a toothbrush and hot water. Get the joint to fit closely together again, binding if necessary. When heating a ring shank for soldering, start at the opposite end to the solder seam; this will cause the metal to expland slightly, pushing the joint closer together.

▲ Use a saw blade to make the joint light-tight. The blade effectively acts as a tiny file, taking a small piece off each side of the joint.

▲ Run a sheet of emery paper through the joint to remove contaminants.

THE PROBLEM

There are small bubbles and pits on the solder joint

Caused by: In its liquid state solder is prone to react with atmospheric gases; when solder solidifies these are trapped as tiny bubbles or small craters. This might be due to the metal or the solder being dirty or too much heat being applied to the solder, or it might follow repeated solderings resulting in the alloys decomposing slightly. This is most apparent when an excessive amount of solder has been used.

THE SOLUTION

Remove excess solder and heat again: Pickle and rinse the piece, then file off any excess solder. Reflux the piece and bind with binding wire if necessary. Heat until the solder flows again; you may judge it necessary to add some more solder.

▲ Pitted solder joint.　　▲ File off excess solder.　　▲ Then reflux and try again.

THE PROBLEM

Links on a chain have become soldered together

Caused by: Sometimes solder can run on to the wrong part of the chain, resulting in two of the links becoming fused together.

THE SOLUTIONS

Use heat to separate the links: Hold one of the fused links in tweezers in a third hand (or enlist a friend to help). Hold the other link while playing a flame over them both. Gently wiggle the link back and forth until it becomes loose. Keep it moving for a while after the flame is removed to make sure that it does not re-solder.

Use a third hand: A third hand is very useful for chain making. Bring both the links on either side of the one to be soldered together and hold them in reverse-action tweezers so that the link to be soldered sticks upright with the joint on top. By doing this, the heat-sinking capability of the tweezers can be used to your advantage and only the part to be soldered is exposed to the flame. A firebrick placed behind the chain will help to reflect the heat back towards the piece being soldered (dispense with this if the flame is very hot).

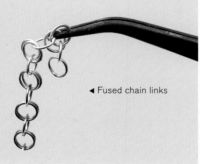

◄ Fused chain links

▲ Using a third hand to hold the chain, heat the links and wiggle them loose.

▲ Make sure previously soldered links are protected from the heat by the tweezers when soldering other links.

THE PROBLEM

Jump rings keep falling off

Caused by: There is not enough of the metal making contact for a stable joint. Reverse-action tweezers might have acted as a heat sink, preventing the jump ring from getting hot enough.

THE SOLUTION

File a flat area and hold with fine tweezers: File a flat area where the jump ring or tubing attaches to the main piece – this will not be discernible once the piece is finished. Use fine stainless steel tweezers to hold the jump ring – these will allow more heat to reach it.

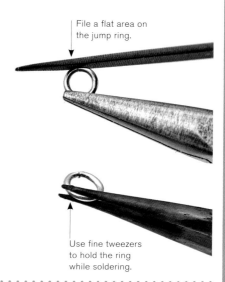

File a flat area on the jump ring.

Use fine tweezers to hold the ring while soldering.

THE PROBLEM

Ear posts or pin backs melt

Caused by: When attaching small or thin pieces of metal to a larger piece, bear in mind that the larger piece will require much more heat to get up to temperature than the tiny pieces. Usually there is no need to heat ear posts or other small pieces at all when soldering them on to something large – they can pick up the ambient heat from the main piece and the hearth. Keep a close eye on the solder and remove heat as soon as it runs.

THE SOLUTION

Remove the melted post or pin and attach a new finding: Hold what is left of the melted post or pin in tweezers, heat until the solder runs and then lift it off. Pickle and rinse the main piece. Any melted solder on the piece can be left and reused. Reflux and position a new finding. When heating, make sure that the larger piece is well heated – it is sometimes useful to put the work on a steel grid on a tripod to allow the heat to get underneath it. Stop as soon as the solder runs.

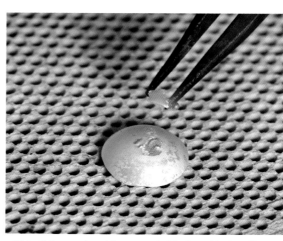

◄ Melted ear post

▲ Pick off the remains of the ear post while the solder is molten.

THE PROBLEM

Rivet has failed; both parts have separated

Caused by: There is not enough folded back on the end of the rivet to grip both sides of the metal together. Either the rivet was too short, it was filed down too far or it slipped down when being upset.

▼ The piece has come apart because the rivet was too short and has failed.

THE SOLUTIONS

Remove and remake with a longer rivet: Remove the rivet and remake it, ensuring that a small amount protrudes from the top and bottom of the piece; this can then be hammered back to hold the metal in place.

Use more rivets or stronger rivets: It might be necessary to add more rivets to secure the pieces together or use a tube rivet, which is stronger.

▶ Rivets can be removed by hammering them out over an indentation in a doming block.

THE PROBLEM

Rivet has bent over and looks messy

Caused by: Rivet was too long and has bent over when being hammered.

Bent rivet

THE SOLUTION

Remove and remake with a shorter rivet: It may be difficult to remove. If necessary, file it right back and use a centre punch over a doming block or open vice to tap out the rivet.

▲ File back the rivet.

▲ Use a centre punch over a doming block to remove it.

▲ Alternatively, place it over an open vice and tap it out.

WHAT'S THE PROBLEM?

SHAPING

DECORATION

WIREWORK

CASTING

STONE SETTING

THE PROBLEM

Rivet was supposed to act like a pivot and allow the other elements to move, but it is shut tight

Caused by: A small space between the metal being joined and the rivet is needed to allow movement.

THE SOLUTIONS

Try to loosen the rivet: It might be possible to loosen the rivet by working it back and forth. Try introducing a lubricant such as liquid detergent to achieve this. If this fails, remove the rivet by drilling through it and then remake.

Temporarily insert thick paper to create a gap: Insert a piece of thick paper between the elements being joined. This can then be burned away, or if the piece cannot be heated, it can be removed by soaking in water and pulling free.

▶ Place some thick paper between the elements to create a gap, then remove the paper afterwards.

THE PROBLEM

Rivet keeps working loose on leather, plastic or other soft material

Caused by: The size of the rivet head cannot cope with the flexibility of the material.

THE SOLUTION

Add some washers: These can form a decorative element and can be any shape, or can be simply a small circle with a hole. They will give the rivet a solid base to attach to and will prevent it from working free.

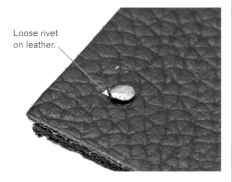

Loose rivet on leather.

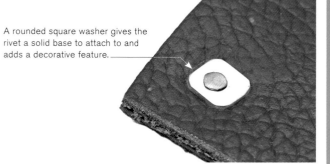

A rounded square washer gives the rivet a solid base to attach to and adds a decorative feature.

THE PROBLEM

Hinges have become frozen together

Caused by: Excess solder has flowed between the hinge knuckles, due to insufficient antiflux or too much solder being used.

THE SOLUTIONS

Use a saw blade to free the hinge: Run a very fine (8/0) saw blade down the hinges. This might be sufficient to free them if there is not too much solder involved.

Remove solder or make new knuckles: If the method above fails, reheat until the solder runs and the pieces can be separated. Unless you are certain that you can remove all the solder from them, it might be safest to make new knuckles. Carefully antiflux the side where you do not want the solder to flow. Position the hinge to face the front so that it will get the most of the direct heat.

▲ A fine saw blade may be enough to free up the hinge.

THE PROBLEM

The piece has become soldered together

Caused by: Excess heat or inadequate use of antiflux has caused the solder to run where it shouldn't be.

THE SOLUTIONS

Use a blade to free the piece: It may be possible to free the two pieces with a fine saw blade (8/0) or by hammering the blade of a utility knife between them.

Heat and remove the solder: If the method above fails, the piece will have to be heated until the solder flows again and then taken apart. All the parts will need to be emery papered to remove any solder that might cause this to happen again. Be lavish with the antiflux the next time.

▲ Try using a fine saw blade to separate the pieces first.

THE PROBLEM

The hinge works but is floppy and loose

Caused by: Hinge pin is too thin.

THE SOLUTION

Use thicker wire for the hinge pin: Remove the hinge pin and select a thicker piece of wire. Hold it in a pin vice and file a tapered point on one end. Stroke the pin with some wax to lubricate it, and then twist it into the knuckles of the hinge. This will have the added bonus of work-hardening the pin as it goes in. It should be a tight fit. Initially the hinge may feel quite stiff, but it will loosen with use.

▲ Twist a thicker lubricated pin into the hinge.

WHAT'S THE PROBLEM?

SHAPING

DECORATION

WIREWORK

CASTING

STONE SETTING

THE PROBLEM

The hinge pin won't fit into tube

Caused by: Knuckles have moved while being soldered and are no longer in alignment, or there may be a burr of metal stuck in the tube; hinge pin might be slightly too wide.

THE SOLUTIONS

Remove obstructions: Using a drill bit held in a pin vice, carefully drill out any obstructions inside the tube.
Fix the alignment: If there is only a slight discrepancy, opening the object or slightly moving it should allow the pin to slide in. If not, try to ascertain which part is out of alignment. Protect all other joints from heat and reposition this knuckle. Use plenty of antiflux to avoid sticking everything together.
File down the hinge pin: If the hinge pin is simply too thick, hold it in a pin vice and file it down while turning it until it fits tightly into the hinge.

▲ Drill out the tube to remove any obstructions.

THE PROBLEM

When closed, the two elements don't align

Caused by: One half may have slipped during construction, or the bearing for the hinge was not properly filed.

THE SOLUTION

Carefully hammer into alignment: If the problem is fairly slight, put the piece on end and lightly hammer the part that protrudes in order to right the pieces. Hammer marks may need to be filed and sanded off. If the slip is very obvious, however, it may be necessary to go back to the beginning.

▲ Hammer back the protruding piece to fix the alignment.

THE PROBLEM

When closed, the edges of the locket don't quite meet perfectly

Caused by: The metal has deformed slightly when being heated.

THE SOLUTION

Exert pressure: Close the hinge and note where the object closes tightly. Open up and insert a fine piece of steel, such as a utility knife blade, on that part. Close the locket and exert some pressure on it. Check to see if the gap has closed. Continue doing this all around until it closes nicely.

▲ Exert pressure on the hinge with a steel blade in place until the hinge will close nicely.

CHAPTER 3

DECORATION

Finishing metal to a high mirror shine is an art that craftspeople can spend years perfecting. Fortunately, it is not the only finishing option open to jewellery designers. Adding texture to work can add another level of interest and variation – and it can cover a multitude of sins. A texture can be as subtle as the imprint made from a piece of cartridge paper, or as impressive as a reticulated mountain range. Adding a patina to work can enhance its graphic qualities or emphasise a texture.

Rolling mill

The rolling mill is an excellent piece of studio equipment. Metal can be milled down to any width; textures can be milled on to sheet; wire and rod can be milled down or tapered. Scrap metal can be smelted and rolled down into serviceable sheet.

The rolling mill is a bit like a steel mangle. The top handle turns to vary the distance between two steel rollers; the handle on the side turns the rollers, compressing the metal that is fed between them. Various roller combinations are available – flat, or with ridges through which wire can be reduced in size. On the outside of the rollers there are usually indentations that roll round wire into D-shaped wire.

More expensive rolling mills have reduction gears that make reducing the thickness of metal much easier and more efficient. The gears reduce the amount of strength required to roll material through the rollers, but you will have to turn the handle more times than if you had no reduction. A reduction of 6–1 means you have to turn the handle six times for the rollers to go around once.

▲ HOLLIE PAXTON
A fine texture has been applied to the milled metal used to form this brooch.

CORRECT USE AND CARE OF THE ROLLING MILL

Never roll ferrous metals in a rolling mill unless the rollers are protected by sandwiching the ferrous metal between two pieces of softer metal.

Always make sure metal is dry before rolling.

Make sure metal is free of borax residue before rolling.

Never press the rollers completely together because any dirt or grit could cause damage.

When the rolling mill is not in use, apply a thin coating of oil to the rollers.

Do not touch the rollers. Oils and acids from your body can damage them, leaving behind small marks and eventually rust.

Sometimes, especially in colleges, bits of masking tape, fabric or plant material can get stuck on the rollers. Remove this by rubbing with wire wool before rolling.

The gears of the roller should be greased every 6 months and the end faces of the rollers should be oiled daily.

Milling down ingots or thick metal

Anneal, pickle, rinse and dry the ingot thoroughly. Judge by eye how wide to set the rollers. The first turn should just make light contact with the ingot to ensure that it is completely flat. Tighten the rollers on subsequent passes so that some resistance can be felt, but it should not be a major struggle to turn the handle. If it is, reverse the metal out and reset the rollers slightly wider apart (a quarter turn of the top handle).

Move the metal through the rollers smoothly, and turn it over end to end after each pass. Don't turn the metal 90 degrees without first annealing it. Anneal as necessary and keep passing through and tightening the rollers until you reach the desired thickness. Sterling silver should be annealed when its gauge has been reduced by half. Always try to keep the handle turning smoothly and regularly; stopping and starting or using a jerky action can result in ridges on the metal.

Using the rolling mill for texture

The pressure of the rollers on annealed metal when sandwiched with paper, fabric, metal meshes or a variety of materials can result in a plethora of interesting textures.

Rolling textures into metal Anneal, pickle, rinse and dry the metal thoroughly. If the texturing material you are using is relatively soft, it can be passed through the rollers on top of a single layer of metal – the shiny metal of the rollers will result in a bright finish against the texture being used. If the texturing material is hard, such as wire, metal mesh or any type of steel, it should be sandwiched between two layers of metal to protect the rollers from damage (it is better to err on the side of caution than risk damaging the rollers). Making a sandwich will result in two pieces of metal with mirror images of the texture, which can be useful when symmetry is required, such as when making earrings.

Judge by eye how far apart the rollers should be set. Take care to align the sample at 90 degrees to the rollers and turn the handle to check the pressure on the piece. If the handle is too hard or too easy to turn, reverse the piece out and adjust the rollers, then try again. Turn the handle smoothly – you only get one chance to apply the texture. The metal will be slightly bent when it comes out, but can be gently tapped flat with a soft mallet.

▲ Sandwich the texturing material between two sheets of metal.

▼ Roll the sandwich through the mill to impress the texture.

Texturing materials A huge variety of dry materials can be used to make impressions. The key to making a good impression is getting the depth of the rolling mill correct for the thickness of metal you are using. It is worth making lots of samples for future reference.

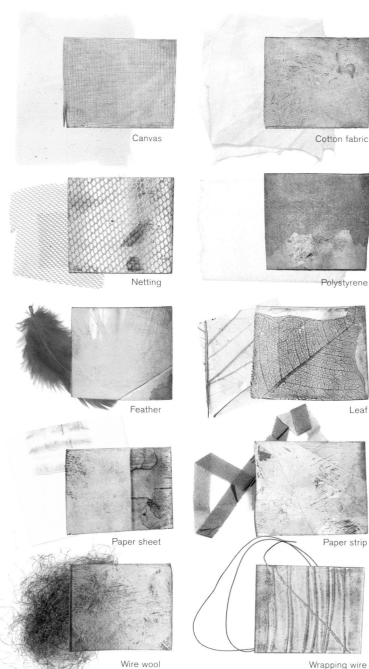

Canvas

Cotton fabric

Netting

Polystyrene

Feather

Leaf

Paper sheet

Paper strip

Wire wool

Wrapping wire

WHAT'S THE PROBLEM?

SHAPING

DECORATION

WIREWORK

CASTING

STONE SETTING

Hammers and punches

Beautiful textures can be introduced to work via hammer strokes and decorative punches. The textures may be used to add contrast to the surface of a piece, or to add small areas of detail or text.

▲ STEPHANIE JOHNSON
Well-placed blows with a creasing hammer give this bangle a beautiful bark-like texture.

The different shaped hammers will all produce a different texture – the tapered face of a cross-peen hammer creates lovely bark-like textures, for example. You can also buy hammers with textured faces. Punches are commercially available in numerous designs, and you can also make your own. Punches with repeated patterns such as lines or crosshatching are known as matting punches.

Rectangular face of a raising hammer

Small, sharp creasing hammer

Small, sharp creasing hammer

Ball end of a small ball-peen hammer

Flat face of a riveting hammer

Hammer with textured face

Leaf-shaped punch

Lined matting punch

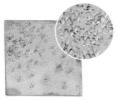

Crosshatched matting punch

Using hammers for texture

Always anneal, pickle and dry the metal before texturing. Make sure the metal is on a smooth, flat surface because the underside can pick up textures when struck; a flat steel plate is good. To minimise the noise, rest this on a sandbag or piece of rubber.

Always try out the effect on a piece of scrap metal first, and experiment with different ways of angling the hammer. The hammer should always be held near the end of the shaft; this makes its use more efficient. Textured surfaces such as lace or sandpaper can be placed on top of the metal and then hammered on to create texture.

The metal may curl up in response to the hammer strokes, so turn it the opposite way on a wooden surface and flatten with a soft mallet. You will get to know the feeling when the piece needs to be re-annealed.

Using punches for texture

As with hammering, metal should be well annealed, pickled and dried. Support the work on a resisting surface, such as an anvil or steel plate. A repoussé hammer is a good choice to use with a punch because its large, flat head means you can concentrate on the business end of the punch and not the end being struck. Sometimes repoussé hammers can be a bit light for punch work, though; a heavier jobbing hammer may be more effective.

As both your hands will be occupied with the punch and the hammer, it is a good idea to tape the metal to the steel plate – masking tape is best for this. Hold the punch perpendicular to the work, with its face making good contact with the metal. Strike the punch firmly with a single blow of the hammer, as multiple strikes can result in a ghostly double image. It is best to practise on scrap metal first in order to gauge the weight of the hammer blow required.

▶ Apply punched text to go around the inside of rings before bending the ring into shape.

Making a punch

You can make your own punches from silver steel, tool steel or even a large steel nail.

1 Acquire some tool steel of an appropriate shape and about 10cm (4in) long. Punches can be square or round in profile. Heat the whole punch with a torch until it is cherry red.

2 Allow it to air cool, then use files, grinders or burrs to create the desired pattern.

3 Reheat the whole punch to cherry red again, and then quench it in water to harden the steel.

4 Check that the shape is correct by pressing it into something soft. Finely sand the whole length of the punch and polish the patterned end.

5 The steel is still not suitable for a lifetime of punching because it would be too brittle, so it needs to be tempered. Rub a little soap on the prepared end, then heat with a torch from the opposite end. As soon as it reaches a straw yellow colour, stop and quench it in water or oil.

Using punches for text

When punching a line of text with letter punches, scribe a faint line where the edge of the punch should be placed. Make sure the punch is the right way up! With punched text, one might as well embrace the higgledy piggledy charm of the technique because it is hard to get the spacing and alignment right. If perfect text is required, engraving or etching might be a better choice.

Texturing rings

Punched or hammered texture can be added to the outside of rings after they have been constructed, which allows the solder line to be covered by the texture. Set the annealed ring on a mandrel in a vice and apply the texture to it. Remember to allow for the taper on the mandrel and turn the ring over regularly. The ring can be taped to the mandrel to keep it in position.

The ring will be enlarged by the percussion, so it should be made several sizes smaller and of a thicker gauge than is finally required. Estimating the amount by which it will stretch can be difficult. It is annoying to apply half the texture and discover that the ring is already too large and thin, so it is better to err on the side of caution and start with quite a thick piece of metal.

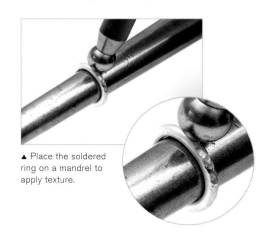

▲ Place the soldered ring on a mandrel to apply texture.

WHAT'S THE PROBLEM?

SHAPING

DECORATION

WIREWORK

CASTING

STONE SETTING

Etching

Etching uses the corrosive nature of acid to remove exposed areas of metal, resulting in a decorative, lightly textured surface that receives patinas well. Areas that have been coated with a resist will remain untouched by the acid and retain their original finish. Nitric acid is most commonly used to etch silver and base metals.

▲ FRIEDA MUNRO
Moth pendant made using
PnP paper as an etch resist.

A resist should be waterproof and impervious to acid, and should adhere well to the metal. A resist such as stop-out varnish (sometimes called black polish) can be painted on and then scratched through to expose the metal, or designs can be painted freehand. Etch-resist pens are useful for finer drawing. Fablon or parcel tape can be used to mask off larger areas. Photographs can be transferred on to PnP (Press-n-Peel) paper or Lazertran paper with a photocopier. Images might need to be reversed and inverted prior to printing – anything black will be the resist, so will remain 'white' or untouched; anything white (or clear) on the image will be etched, so you do have to think in reverse.

Some precious metals, such as pure gold and platinum, do not react with nitric acid, although pure gold does react with aqua regia, a mixture of concentrated nitric acid and hydrochloric acid. This technique is rarely used nowadays because of the high price of these metals.

Making etching solutions

Choose the vessel you intend to use as an etching bath – a shallow glass baking dish is a good option. Measure out the total volume required for this dish in water first – if the piece to be etched is a flat sheet, you should only need the solution to be a centimetre or so deep. This makes it simple to calculate how much acid to add.

Refer to the chart below for the correct concentrations of acid to water for various materials. Have a funnel on hand to make transferring the mix to a suitable bottle easy. This is best done in a sink so that any spillages can be flushed away. Once mixed, the solution can be stored (see safety notes on page 171) and reused many times.

How to etch metal

Always ensure metals are thoroughly degreased before applying a resist. A dab of pumice powder on a toothbrush is good for this, then rinse and dry carefully. Rinsing and pickling will also degrease metal. Giving a final wipe with acetone or rubbing alcohol provides extra grease elimination. Even the grease from your fingers can impair etching, so wear latex gloves or remember to hold the metal carefully by its edge. You can tell if metal has been properly degreased because water will sit over the metal in a smooth sheet – anywhere that resists the water is still slightly greasy.

MATERIAL	SOLUTION
Base metals – copper, brass, gilding metal	One part nitric acid (70 per cent reagent grade) to one part water
Silver	One part nitric acid to three parts water
Steel	One part nitric acid to six parts distilled water
Natural materials – bone, ivory, shell	One part nitric acid to five parts water

▶ Degrease the metal thoroughly.

Using stop-out varnish

Various materials can be used as a resist – stop-out varnish, sticky-backed plastic, parcel tape, natural resin (aquatint), PnP paper, Lazertran paper – basically, anything that prevents the acid from touching the metal. Cover any parts that you do not want to etch with parcel tape, including the sides of the metal. Make sure any resist used is properly dry before use.

▲ The finished results.

1 Paint the metal with stop-out varnish.

2 Apply the required design. For example, scratch out a design using a steel point.

3 Try feathering the edges of the stop-out varnish to create the design.

4 You can also paint the design with broad brushstrokes.

5 Pour the acid mix into a shallow glass bowl and submerge the piece in it. Bubbles will form on the surface; these can be brushed off with a feather.

6 Check the piece frequently to see how deep the etch is (doing a small test square first is a good idea). A slow etch is more accurate; aggressive etching can lead to undercuts in the pattern. Use a sample piece to estimate etching time. Keep an eye on the resist to make sure it is not coming away from the metal. If it is, rinse the piece thoroughly and dry carefully, then reapply the resist where required.

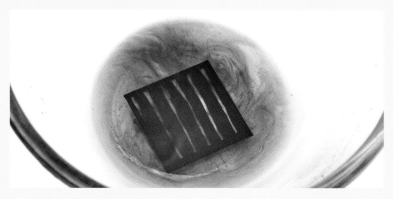

7 Once etching is complete, remove from the acid and rinse thoroughly. It is a good idea to remove any packing tape under running water because occasionally acid can be trapped in its folds. The resist can be removed by heating gently or submerging in acetone or white spirit, depending on the resist used.

WHAT'S THE PROBLEM?

SHAPING

DECORATION

WIREWORK

CASTING

STONE SETTING

Using PnP paper

PnP (Press-n-Peel) paper is a blue plastic film, shiny on one side and matt on the other. Images should be high-contrast black and white. The image should be reversed out, and any letters or numbers should be a mirror image. Print a whole sheet of images at a time as the paper will not go through the copier after cutting.

1 Photocopy or print on to the matt side of the paper. If your printer has the option to select 'transparency' as the medium, use it – it puts a good thick layer of ink on the paper. Cut out the required image.

2 A flat surface such as a sheet of medium-density fiberboard (MDF) is a good base for applying PnP. Heat an iron to a medium/hot setting – 135–160°C (275–325°F) but not a steam setting – and warm up the MDF. Place the PnP, image side down, on to the metal and cover with a sheet of plain paper.

3 Iron over it using a circular motion. Keep going until the image shows clearly through the back of the PnP paper. If you have one, you can pass the piece through a laminator several times, which heats the metal evenly.

4 Allow the metal to air cool and then carefully peel back the PnP paper. Sometimes small holes are left; these can be filled with stop-out varnish. Complete the etching process (see page 91).

Using Lazertran

Lazertran is similar to a temporary tattoo – a white backing paper holds a water-release decal. Copy the image in black and white using a colour photocopier or laser printer on to a sheet of Lazertran. As with PnP paper, use the 'transparency' setting if available on your printer.

1 To ensure that the toner is fully melted on to the paper, put the sheet into a hot oven or heat it with a hair dryer. In a short time the black toner will go shiny. This will avoid bubbles forming later in the method. Cut out the required image.

2 Soak the image in water for a minute or so to release the transfer.

3 Place the transfer, image side down, on to the degreased metal. Using a soft rubber squeegee, a finger or paper towel, gently rub from the centre outwards to expel all air bubbles, creases and moisture.

4 Slide off the backing paper and dry the piece carefully with paper towel. Put it in a domestic oven with the heat at its lowest setting for an hour. After that, increase the temperature every 15 minutes until you get up to 200°C (390°F). The black image should be glossy and slightly raised.

5 Wash away the clear part of the decal using isopropyl alcohol, leaving only the toners on the metal. Wash off the alcohol in warm soapy water. Fill gaps with stop-out varnish, then complete the etching process (see page 91). After etching, remove the toner with solvent or by heating gently.

WHAT'S THE PROBLEM?

SHAPING

DECORATION

WIREWORK

CASTING

STONE SETTING

Reticulation

When the surface of a sheet of metal is melted, a rippled texture is formed. Copper alloys, Britannia silver and gold can be reticulated, but it is most commonly practised on sterling silver.

▲ FRIEDA MUNRO
The use of reticulated metal to make simple band rings means that each ring will be slightly different.

As prepared silver heats up, the difference in melting temperatures creates tension as the copper-rich bottom layer melts but the pure silver top layer does not. As the flame moves on and the copper layer contracts and hardens, the fine silver conforms to it, creating a wrinkled surface. The effect can be quite unpredictable; practice will help you know when to stop and when to push the metal further.

How to reticulate sterling silver

Reticulation is best carried out on metal of over 18 gauge (1mm) because thinner sheets are more inclined to melt and form holes. Make sure the sheet is flat. Decide in advance whether the edges will be pierced afterwards (this can create a good contrast with the reticulated surface) or left as they are. The edges can pull in slightly when being reticulated.

Preparation Anneal and pickle the metal, then scrub with a brass brush. Heat up and pickle the metal at least five more times; do not exceed annealing temperature when doing this. This will raise a layer of pure silver to the surface

of the metal (this is the white bloom you get on pickled metal when copper has been depleted from the alloy). Rinse the pickle off the metal before reheating each time.

Heating the metal Place the prepared metal on a clean, flat surface. A charcoal block is good for this because it retains heat well. Bring the metal rapidly up to heat. Use two torches if you have them, one with a large, slightly bushy flame to hold the metal at the correct temperature, and the other with a smaller, hotter flame to push the melted metal around. Heat the metal until it is beyond annealing temperature, when it is bright orange and starting to liquefy.

Starting at one end of the sheet, play the hotter torch around on the surface of the metal while holding the larger flame slightly farther away. The more heat that is applied, the higher the ridges will be. If you only have one torch, alternate between a large bushy flame to get the piece to temperature, then turn down the power and move the head of the torch closer to the metal to direct the heat.

Areas of the metal can be protected from reticulation by coating them with heat protection paste. Be aware that reticulated metal is often rather brittle and more porous.

▲ Heat the metal at least six times without exceeding annealing temperature.

▲ Pickle and rinse between each reheating.

▲ Hold the hotter flame close to the metal.

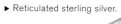

▶ Reticulated sterling silver.

Plating

Plating is an excellent way to vary the colour of your work – pieces made in base metal can be transformed into gold or silver, and silver can become gold. It can be a great way to test out a collection without spending a fortune.

White gold jewellery is often plated with rhodium to give it a bright white finish. Rhodium and ruthenium can also be used to give a black finish. Getting an object plated should be the last part of the making process – plating will only change the colour of the piece, not the finish. If a matt piece of work is plated, it will not become shiny. Plating simply coats the piece in a couple of microns of another metal. Polishing after plating will wear the thin layer of precious metal off it.

▶ FRIEDA MUNRO
Many jewellery collections offer pieces in gold plate or silver.

Plating practicalities

Plating will eventually wear off on pieces of jewellery that are exposed to friction, such as rings or bracelets. You can specify the thickness of plate – 6 microns is a good thickness for rings; 2 microns is sufficient for pieces such as earrings and necklaces. You can also specify that pieces be flash-plated – that is, plated with a very thin layer of precious metal. This is useful if testing colours for a collection, or if a very small adjustment has been made to a piece resulting in a small loss of plate.

It is possible to mask off areas of a piece prior to plating so that the original metal colour will be retained. The stop-off is called Lacomit and is similar to nail varnish; after plating it can be removed with Lacomit remover (acetone). Occasionally some of the plate colour may bleed through under the Lacomit, so apply two coats, allowing each to dry completely.

Professional plating service

Some jewellery studios keep a small plating unit, but because of the noxious chemicals involved and the large outlay of having to buy the expensive gold solution, most jewellers send their plating out to the experts.

The best way to find a good plater is to speak to other makers and find out who they recommend. Some platers will offer different colours of gold such as green or rose gold; some might have a large minimum charge. It is worth forging a close relationship with your plater. They can advice you on how best to prepare work for plating. Some prefer large volumes of work to be wired up – that is, attached to fine copper wire so that they can be suspended easily in the plating solution – but others prefer to do this themselves. Prices vary considerably and are also dependent on the market price of gold.

Many platers offer a polishing service that is particularly useful if you need a flawless mirror polish on your work. If you are making batches of jewellery or designing a whole collection, it is best to get all the work plated at the same time because colours can vary slightly from batch to batch.

▲ KELLY McCALLUM
The striking gold-plated insect against the desaturated tones of pearls and silver works to great effect in this brooch.

▲ ALEX MONROE
Areas of the daisies have been 'stopped out' with Lacomit to prevent them from plating.

WHAT'S THE PROBLEM?

SHAPING

DECORATION

WIREWORK

CASTING

STONE SETTING

Patination

A patina is a fine layer on the surface of a metal resulting from a chemical change in the alloy. Patinas will usually occur naturally over time due to exposure to air, known as oxidisation. These processes can be accelerated by the use of various chemicals and techniques.

► CJ POUPAZIS
The subtle grey tones in this brooch have been achieved using liver of sulphur.

Copper takes colour very readily. Substances such as lemon juice and vinegar will colour copper over time to create verdigris – think of copper roofs. Most metals also go through a rainbow of colours when gently heated. The effect will vary depending on how the patina is applied. It can be painted on, dipped, spattered or sponged, and metal can be smothered in sawdust soaked in a patina solution for a mottled effect.

Chemicals such as cupric nitrate or ferric nitrate can be mixed with water and applied to warm metal in a well-ventilated space to achieve bright blue or rusty red colours. There are several antiquing fluids that work well on base metals, turning them black or dark brown. Areas can then be rubbed back, leaving recesses and etched or engraved areas black.

Silver can be turned black or gun-metal grey with Platinol, liver of sulphur or various other commercially available antiquing fluids also known as oxidising agents (although they don't actually oxidise at all). The colours of black vary slightly between these products. Platinol produces a reliable black/dark grey colour on silver; liver of sulphur can produce a variety of colours as it is applied.

Practicalities

Oxidising agents generally smell awful due to their sulphurous nature, so always work in a well-ventilated area and protect eyes and hands. Before applying a patina to a finished piece, it is worth doing several tests and keeping notes of the effects to see which one works best.

Before applying any type of patina, metals should be degreased either by heating, pickling

and rinsing, or by applying a mixture of pumice and detergent on a brush. You can tell when a piece of metal has been properly degreased because water will not ball up on the surface, but will cover it in a sheet. Areas of the metal can be masked off so that the patina will not reach them to provide contrast – tape, wax or wood glue will all work.

Preserving the patina Patina layers are quite thin and delicate, so are not suitable for pieces that will be exposed to any wear. They should be applied at the end of the making process for this reason. They can be preserved to an extent by applying a layer of wax, jade oil or clear lacquer over the top. Renaissance wax, beeswax or furniture wax creates a good lustre and preserves patinas well. Wax will darken black patinas, but is unsuitable for verdigris and deadens refractory colours on heat patinas. Apply wax liberally with a soft cloth. Clear laquer can be sprayed or painted on to the piece – it has to be very clean and dry for this to work.

◄ FRIEDA MUNRO
The gold-plated tail of the fox contrasts with the oxidised silhouette.

Black/grey patinas

Commercially available oxidising solutions such as Platinol are very effective in quickly turning metals black. Platinol works well on copper, but turns brass a brown colour. It can be diluted to make the effect more controllable. Only use nylon brushes with Platinol because it destroys bristle ones. For this reason take care to protect eyes and hands when using it, and work in a well-ventilated area.

▲ The finished piece.

▲ JESSICA DE LOTZ
The oxidised surface of the concierge bell ring is in striking contrast with its pale-coloured holder.

Applying Platinol

1 Make sure that the metal is entirely grease-free. Degrease using a toothbrush and pumice, for example.

2 Paint on the Platinol with a nylon-bristled brush or a cotton swab; the metal should turn black right away.

3 Rinse and brush lightly, then dry and reapply the patina to ensure an even coating. Rinse again. Pieces can also be dipped briefly in the solution to coat them.

4 On silver the patina can be burnished into the metal by putting the piece into a barrel polisher for a short time or the surface patina can be removed, leaving only recessed detail black.

Liver of sulphur

Liver of sulphur, also known as potassium sulphide, comes in lump form. It should be double-sealed in an airtight container and stored in a cool, dark place. It smells strongly of sulphur so should be used in a well-ventilated space. To use, dissolve a teaspoonful of liver of sulphur in 200ml (7fl oz) of boiling water and suspend the piece to be patinated in the liquid. Keep it immersed until it reaches the right colour, then remove and rinse thoroughly under a cold running tap. If using with copper, make up a weaker solution and brass brush the piece after each dipping. Liver of sulphur can also produce a range of colours in silver using the following method.

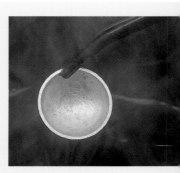

1 Have a pan of hot water nearby and two cold water rinses. Heat the liver of sulphur mixture to about 60°C (150°F). Heat the degreased metal piece in the hot water and then suspend in the liver of sulphur mixture.

WHAT'S THE PROBLEM?

SHAPING

DECORATION

WIREWORK

CASTING

STONE SETTING

Blue/green patinas

Vinegar/ammonia/sawdust Fill a resealable box with sawdust. Mix together one part vinegar to three parts ammonia and dampen the sawdust with it. Bury a piece of well-degreased copper in the sawdust and leave for between an hour and 2 days, depending on the depth of patina required. If you don't have any sawdust, experiment with other substances – paper towel or cheesecloth can leave interesting marks on the metal.

Ammonia/salt Make a fume chamber – a large plastic yoghurt container with a removable lid works well. Drill two holes on each side about halfway down to allow two pieces of wire to act as a shelf for the piece of copper. Dampen a paper towel with ammonia. Cover a piece of degreased copper with salt, then dampen the salt with water or vinegar. Put the lid on and leave for between an hour and 2 days to let the patina develop.

Cupric nitrate Dissolve 200g (7oz) of copper nitrate crystals in 1 litre (2 pints) of warm water to make cupric nitrate solution. Put the prepared metal on to a heatproof mat, paint with the solution and then gently heat it with a torch flame to develop the colour. As the water evaporates a blue/green residue remains. Take care not to burn the residue or it will go black. Continue to reapply the solution to achieve the required patina.

◄ Copper patinated using vinegar, ammonia and sawdust.

◄ Copper patinated using ammonia, salt and vinegar.

▲ Building up cupric nitrate patina gradually on warm metal.

2 Watch carefully for the required colour to develop. Metal goes deep black very quickly.

3 Immediately take it out and plunge in one cold water bath, then the other, to arrest the process.

4 Colours tend to start with light gold. Dip in solution very briefly for a golden colour.

5 With practice (and luck) a spectrum of colours can be achieved on silver by dipping in solution for different lengths of time, moving from gold into reds, purples, blues and greens, ending up in grey/black.

Red/brown patinas

Copper plating This is something that jewellers usually try to avoid, but contaminating used pickle with steel and allowing copper molecules to be deposited on metal will turn any metal pink. It only works if you are using pickle that has some copper in it – the pickle should be a blue colour. If you are using brand new pickle, leave a couple of bits of copper in it overnight. Put the metal to be plated in the pickle tank and add some steel – try binding wire or old saw blades. This can be a very useful technique to get brass to accept a patina – the fine layer of copper deposited on the surface with this technique will respond more readily to patinas than brass will.

Ferric nitrate Dissolve 15g (½oz) of ferric nitrate in 500ml (1 pint) of warm water. Apply in the same way as cupric nitrate, heating the metal gently and painting the patina solution on. It will turn the metal a rusty orange colour.

Bicarbonate of soda For a brown patina, mix bicarbonate of soda in a spray bottle half full of hot water until additional bicarbonate of soda will not dissolve. Spray on to the prepared copper, allow to air dry and then repeat as often as necessary.

▲ Copper-plated brass   ▲ Copper-plated silver

▲ Building up ferric nitrate patina gradually on warm metal.

Heat patinas

Copper responds best to being heated, turning a variety of colours including deep red and purple. Degrease the piece of copper and then paint both sides with borax paste. Heat with a strong hot flame until the metal glows orange, then turn it over and repeat. Quench in hot water and pickle briefly. Repeat if necessary.

Refractory metals such as titanium can display a huge array of colours when exposed to heat, or when anodised electrically in the case of niobium. They are quite hard to work with and cannot be soldered or easily worked. In the case of aluminium, the anodising process forms a layer of aluminium oxide, or corundum, which is very hard, relatively inert, electrically insulating and can absorb dyes easily.

◄ Copper with heat patina and finished with Renaissance wax.

◄ Laser engraving of a cloud on blue aluminium.

▲ Copper + Platinol

▲ Brass + Platinol

▲ Copper + liver of sulphur

▲ Brass + liver of sulphur

▲ Copper + ferric nitrate

▲ Brass + ferric nitrate

▲ Copper + cupric nitrate

▲ Brass + cupric nitrate

▲ Copper + sawdust/ammonia

▲ Brass + sawdust/ammonia

▲ Copper + ammonia/salt

▲ Brass + ammonia/salt

▲ Copper + heat patina

▲ Brass + heat patina

WHAT'S THE PROBLEM?

SHAPING

DECORATION

WIREWORK

CASTING

STONE SETTING

Polishing

Generally, the final stage in the making process is applying the surface finish. A high polish can radically change a piece of jewellery, but the finish does not have to be super shiny. Often the contrast between matt and shiny can be very striking.

▲ STEPHANIE JOHNSON
The burnished edge of the metal adds a seductive gleam to the earrings.

There are polishing mops and compounds that impart various subtle satin finishes, stippled biscuit-like finishes or scratched surfaces on metal. The best high finishes are achieved using a polishing motor and polishing compounds, but jewellery can also be polished with a barrel polisher or a magnetic pin barrel, as well as by hand.

▲ Selection of polishing mops.

▶ Texturing mops are available to impart various grades of satin finish.

▶ Mops with steel wires radiating from them can impart a stippled texture.

◀ Tripoli

▲ Rouge

Polishing motors and mops

Polishing motors are expensive and create a lot of mess, so are generally only used in colleges and larger workshops. For a small workshop, there are small mops that fit in a micromotor or pendant drill. The polishing procedure is the same in both instances.

Different mops are available for polishing motors – calico for the first stage of polishing (these are more rugged), and swansdown or fluffy wool for a final polish. Synthetic suede mops are now available. The mops usually have a leather centre and screw on to the spindle on the polishing machine.

When using a polishing motor, hair should be tied back and any long necklaces or scarves removed. Goggles and masks should be worn, but not gloves as they could get trapped in the spindle.

Polishing compounds

There are lots of polishing compounds available. Tripoli is a coarse brown compound containing silica that imparts a satin finish. Rouge is a fine red compound that imparts a mirror shine. Luxi is a water-based, animal fat-free, silica-free compound that comes in various grades.

It is important that each compound is used on a separate mop – getting some coarse compound on a rouge mop will mean the finish will never be as good as it could be. The piece of jewellery should be scrubbed with very hot water and liquid detergent to remove all traces of the rough compound before moving on to the next stage.

Polishing on a motor

Tie hair back and put on goggles and a mask. Start the motor running with the appropriate mop in place. Push some of the polishing medium on to the mop (start with tripoli, or some other coarse compound). Make sure it is well coated. Holding the piece of jewellery in both hands, push it on to the mop and keep the piece moving about. Don't push too hard. The first stage can be very abrasive and can easily obliterate details that you might want to keep. Be aware that the work can get very hot because of the friction. Scrub off any excess compound with hot water and

WHAT'S THE PROBLEM?

SHAPING

DECORATION

WIREWORK

CASTING

STONE SETTING

Preparing the piece for polishing

Polishing should only be carried out after other surface refining techniques have been used on the piece.

1 Use the appropriate files to remove solder or saw marks and to smooth contours.

2 With emery paper, work up through the grades to remove file marks and small scratches. Small pieces of emery paper can be wrapped around needle files to get into hard-to-reach places.

3 Rubber burrs in various shapes and grades are available for the micromotor. These can take the place of emery paper and achieve a faster result.

4 Polishing threads are strings that can be attached to the workbench and used to get into really hard-to-reach areas, such as stone settings or holes.

▲ Polishing with tripoli on a motor.

liquid detergent, then inspect the piece. It should have a uniform satin finish. Repeat the process on a soft mop with rouge or an equivalent high-polish compound. Once cleaned, the piece should have a mirror finish. If scratches are revealed, go back to the emery stage.

Using a barrel polisher

Barrel polishers tumble pieces of jewellery around in a chamber containing steel spheres and rods known as shot, along with water and polishing powder. They are useful for

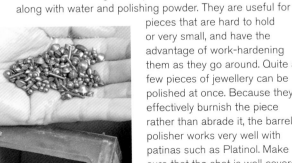

pieces that are hard to hold or very small, and have the advantage of work-hardening them as they go around. Quite a few pieces of jewellery can be polished at once. Because they effectively burnish the piece rather than abrade it, the barrel polisher works very well with patinas such as Platinol. Make sure that the shot is well covered

▲ Steel shot

with clean water and add a tablespoonful of barrel polishing soap. The time it will take to polish depends on the speed that the machine rotates at. Check it after 15 minutes. If barrelled for too long, fine detail can be lost. Always leave soap and water in the barrel polisher to prevent the steel shot from rusting.

Hand polishing

Hand polishing tools can be made by gluing a piece of leather, suede side up, on to a buff stick. These can be used with tripoli or rouge to hand polish work. Another option is Gariflex, a block of soft rubber containing abrasive grains. It comes in three grades and generates a good satin finish. Scotchbrite, the green nylon cloth used for cleaning pots and pans, also imparts a good satin finish.

► Use a buff stick and rouge to polish by hand.

THE PROBLEM

There are marks on my work

Caused by: The rollers might have dirt on them, or some other damage.

THE SOLUTIONS

Clean the rollers: Check that the rollers are clean and that no tape or debris has been left on them. Wipe them with wire wool to clean them. It is important that the rollers never touch each other because bits of dirt, grit or other contaminants can cause damage.

Avoid damaged area or repair rollers: If you are very unlucky, someone might have damaged the rollers by putting a steel object in them. If the damage only affects a small area, get into the habit of avoiding it. If it is a long mark, all that can be done is to send the rollers to be re-machined or buy new ones.

▲ Marks on metal from rollers.

▲ Masking tape stuck to rollers.

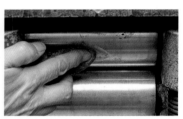

▲ Clean the rollers with wire wool.

THE PROBLEM

The texture I tried to apply is not very clear

Caused by: The rollers might not be close enough, the metal might not have been properly annealed or the texturing material being used is not robust enough to leave a decent impression.

THE SOLUTIONS

Re-anneal and try again: Re-anneal the metal and pass it through the mill again with the rollers set slightly closer together.

Choose a different material:
■ Relatively crisp texturing materials work best – for example, nylon lace gives a better impression than cotton – although even fine, subtle elements like tissue paper or hair can make beautiful textures.

■ Fresh leaves just turn to mush, but the leaf skeletons available from craft shops leave a great impression.
■ Feathers are very effective, although the central spine can dominate the subtlety of the fine fronds.
■ Doilies or paper cutouts can create a lovely contrast between matt and shiny finishes. Areas that stand out will create an intaglio effect on the metal; holes in the texturing material will result in raised areas on the metal.

▶ Linen

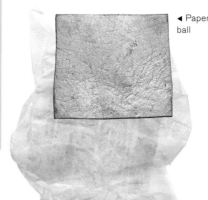

◀ Paper ball

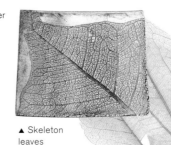

▲ Skeleton leaves

WHAT'S THE PROBLEM?

SHAPING

DECORATION

WIREWORK

CASTING

STONE SETTING

THE PROBLEM

Metal has become misshapen

▲ Rhombus shape   ▲ Banana shape   ▲ Bumpy

THE CAUSES

Square went in but rhombus came out: The metal was not inserted perpendicular to the rollers and has deformed under pressure.

Metal is now bent like a banana on one side: It might not have been fed perpendicular into the rollers, or the rollers may be set unevenly.

Sheet is bumpy and will not lie flat: Metal has been put under too much pressure too quickly or has been under-annealed.

THE SOLUTIONS

Rhombus: Trim the metal true or start again with a fresh piece.

Banana:
■ Hold the metal perpendicular to the bench, with the two end points touching the wood and the outward-curving edge upwards, and gently hammer the middle of the curved edge with a soft mallet until it straightens. Lay the metal flat and use a mallet to flatten it.

■ Move the rollers until they almost touch. Check that the gap is even and not wider at one side than the other. If the rollers need to be adjusted, check the user manual that came with the mill.

Bumpy: Re-anneal and roll again a few times before tightening the rollers any further. Only tighten by a quarter turn (anticlockwise) at a time.

▲ Use a square to mark 90-degree angles and trim true.

▲ Use a mallet to square up and flatten the metal.

THE PROBLEM

The edge of the metal is cracking

Caused by: The metal has been under-annealed.

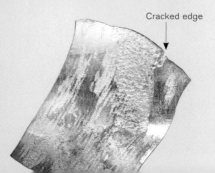

Cracked edge

THE SOLUTIONS

Trim and try again: Cut off the cracked piece, then anneal again and re-roll.

Start again: Start again with a fresh piece of metal, making sure that you anneal it to the correct temperature (see page 40). Pickle after annealing and then roll through the mill.

▲ Anneal the metal to the correct temperature.

▶ Pickle after annealing, and then roll through the mill.

Hammers and punches

THE PROBLEM

Can an unsatisfactory homemade punch be reformed after being tempered?

Caused by: Sometimes a punch is just not the right design for the job, and it can take repeated use of a punch to realise that a shape is not quite right. If the punch is deteriorating with use, such as the textured pattern flaking off, this means that the punch has been under-tempered and is brittle.

THE SOLUTION

Heat, reshape and re-temper: Heat the punch until it is cherry red. Allow it to air cool and then reshape the end. Heat again until cherry red, then quench and sand it down. Re-temper the steel, heating gently from the non-punching end until a straw colour appears – this happens at quite a low temperature. Then quench in water or oil.

▲ Use a file to reshape the punch as required.

▲ Gently heat the tool from the non-punching end to re-temper it.

◀ The steel is tempered when it reaches this straw colour.

THE PROBLEM

Punch mark is unclear on one side

Caused by: The punch has not been held at 90 degrees to the metal or has been hammered at an angle.

THE SOLUTIONS

Flatten the mistake: If the impression is fairly light, it may be possible to planish the metal flat again with a planishing hammer or sand the area back. This area will now be work-hardened, so re-anneal before continuing.

Reposition and try again: If the impression is quite deep, you may be able, with care, to reposition the punch and strike it again.

▲ Flatten the mistake with a hammer.

▲ Sand back the area.

▲ Flood with solder and then re-sand if necessary.

WHAT'S THE PROBLEM?

SHAPING

DECORATION

WIREWORK

CASTING

STONE SETTING

THE PROBLEM

Hammering a texture on the metal has resulted in it becoming very thin

Caused by: Hammer blows will make metal thinner and of a larger surface area. The direction in which the metal stretches is determined by the shape of the hammer head.

THE SOLUTION

Make test pieces first: Practise any hammered texture on scrap metal before moving on to a final piece. It can be hard to estimate how far metal will stretch in relation to its initial thickness and the amount of hammer blows required to achieve the desired texture.

Once metal has become thin, it is impossible to thicken it up. It also tends to warp, so it is difficult to sweat solder it on to another piece of metal. Small pieces may be used for another project, or it may just have to be scrapped.

▲ Metal too thin after applying hammered texture.

THE PROBLEM

Ring has become too large and texturing isn't finished

Caused by: It is hard to estimate how far a ring might stretch.

THE SOLUTION

Remove a section of the ring: Saw the ring open near the solder joint, then cut out a couple of millimetres on the other side of the seam (estimate this in relation to how much hammering is left to do). Re-solder, pickle and continue.

▲ Cut out a piece of the ring at the solder seam, then continue.

THE PROBLEM

Spelling mistake or letter upside down

Caused by: Sometimes one is concentrating so hard on getting the punch straight and the hammer blow correct, that mistakes get made.

Spelling error

THE SOLUTIONS

Abrade the area: It may be possible to file and emery the mistake away and then re-punch it.
Fill with solder: If the above solution is not possible and you are working with silver, carry on with the piece until it is up to the polishing stage or prior to stone setting. Flood the mistake with solder (this is not a practical solution for base metal, as the solder will show). Take care to antiflux thoroughly any areas where the solder should not flow and try to keep the flux only on the part to be filled. Protect any soldered seams with a heat protection paste. If possible, use hard solder

as this has the colour closest to the metal. Heat until the solder runs, then pickle, dry and punch again (carefully).

▲ Flood the error with solder, sand down and reapply the letter the right way up.

THE PROBLEM

The etching is deep but the edges are blurry

Caused by: The solution is quite strong and active and this has caused the resist to be undercut. The resist might not have dried properly or might have been too thin at the edges.

▶ Blurry edges

THE SOLUTIONS

Dilute and start again: Once this has happened, the only thing to do is start again. Dilute the solution further and allow longer for the metal to etch more accurately. If you are working with very fine detail, it is worth letting it etch more slowly. Conduct test pieces to obtain the best solution for clarity.

Pay attention: Take more care when applying the resist. If you pay close attention to the etching process, you should be able to spot the resist failing as soon as it happens and minimise the damage.

▲ Make test pieces using different strength solutions and timings.

THE PROBLEM

PnP image is not transferring properly

Caused by: The ink did not release properly because it did not get hot enough.

▶ Poorly transferred image

THE SOLUTION

Heat the metal first: Put the metal on a hotplate for a few minutes or lay it on the surface of the iron. Then set the iron to its hottest setting, move the hot metal to a clean flat surface, place a piece of clean paper over the transfer and iron all over. Lift off the PnP film when you can see the black image showing clearly through the blue paper.

▶ The transfer is ready when the black image shows clearly through the blue paper.

THE PROBLEM

The PnP image has gone black

Caused by: It has been ironed for too long and the image has melted into a single blob.

◀ Over-ironed PnP image

THE SOLUTION

Always print extra images: Clean off the ruined black image with white spirit and iron on a new one.

▼ Use white spirit to clean off the PnP and reapply.

WHAT'S THE PROBLEM?

SHAPING

DECORATION

WIREWORK

CASTING

STONE SETTING

THE PROBLEM

The resist is flaking off

Caused by: The metal might not have been properly degreased, causing the resist to come off. The PnP paper may not have been adequately heated to bond to metal, or the acid might be too strong.

THE SOLUTIONS

Reapply: Remove from the acid as soon as you notice the resist coming off. Rinse well, dry and reapply stop-out varnish as necessary.

Dilute the acid: If the acid seemed to be very active, try diluting it a bit before reapplying as above.

▶ Use a paintbrush to reapply the resist to the flaked off or missing areas.

THE PROBLEM

The image is reversed

Caused by: When using photographic images or just painting resist on metal, you have to think in reverse. Anything not protected from the acid will appear darker (this can be enhanced with oxidising agents).

THE SOLUTIONS

Create a photo negative: If using a photographic image, it should be reversed to make a 'photo negative'. Remember that any text should be mirrored. This is most easily achieved in an image-editing package such as Photoshop.
Reverse in a photocopier: An image can be reversed by copying it on to acetate and placing this the other way up in a photocopier.

▲ Positive image

▲ Negative image

THE PROBLEM

A fresh batch of acid is working very slowly

Caused by: Acid solutions tend to get more active as they are used (obviously this tails off eventually).

THE SOLUTION

Save some old solution: It is worth keeping a small amount of the old solution to kick-start the new batch.

◀ Save some old solution in a clearly labelled bottle.

Reticulation

THE PROBLEM

Difficulty getting the desired effect

Caused by: Reticulation tends to be unpredictable, although practice does pay off as you get more sensitive to the behaviour of the molten metal. Drafts of air can affect reticulation. Reticulation also often results in firestain because of the successive heatings.

THE SOLUTIONS

Control the temperature: Try using different torches if you can. Build firebricks around the piece to minimise drafts.

Cover or remove firestain: The surface detail means that abrasive means of removal are unsuitable. Cover with silver or gold plating, or remove firestain by bright dipping (see page 67).

▲ Use firebricks to protect against drafts.

▲ Use bright dipping to remove firestain.

THE PROBLEM

The piece has shrunk a lot or a hole has appeared

Caused by: If the piece overheats, the molten metal may pool at the centre, causing edges to shink inwards. Too much heat applied to one area can cause it to melt through.

THE SOLUTION

Remake allowing for shrinkage: The piece might have been too thin to start with, so try using a thicker gauge of metal. Use the failed piece for future projects.
Redesign your piece: Try to redesign the piece to incorporate a negative space, or use it as an opportunity for setting a stone into the piece.

▼ Use the hole in the reticulated silver as a stone setting.

THE PROBLEM

The underside has also reticulated and is bumpy

Caused by: The metal has been pushed into dramatic ridges. This probably gives the desired effect on the front of the piece, but not so much on the reverse.

THE SOLUTIONS

Set the reticulated piece: If you need the underside of the piece to be smooth, try setting the reticulated metal into a bezel as you would a stone.
Add a lining: If it is being used as a ring, make a smooth lining that fits the ring tightly, then flare the ends back on a couple of doming punches.

▲ Add a smooth inner lining to a reticulated ring.

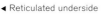

◄ Reticulated underside

fix-its

Plating

THE PROBLEM

The finish on the metal is matt. Is there any way to change it after plating?

Caused by: The final finish may have been overlooked, or you might have had a change of heart on seeing it.

THE SOLUTIONS

Barrel polish briefly: Any polishing done after plating will remove the plate. A non-reductive polishing technique like barrel polishing might brighten it up a little, but don't leave it in too long.
Polish and replate: The only other option is to polish the piece to the required finish and have it replated. If it only affects a small area, you could get the piece flash-plated with a thin layer of metal. Areas that have retained their plate could also be Lacomited, leaving only the unplated area visible for replating.

▲ Copper ring with a matt finish.

▲ The matt finish is not disguised by the gold plating.

THE PROBLEM

Plating has come back looking patchy

Caused by: This may have occurred when the work was being dried after plating.

THE SOLUTIONS

Clean it and barrel polish: Rub gently with a silver cloth. If that fails, try scrubbing it gently with liquid detergent and a soft toothbrush, then rinse well and dry carefully with a soft cloth. Barrel polish it for a very short time.
Return to plater: If it is still patchy, return it to the plating company.

▲ Try cleaning it with a silver cloth.

THE PROBLEM

How can plate be removed from a piece?

Caused by: You might decide that the plated colour does not work with the piece and wish to restore it to its original colour.

THE SOLUTIONS

Plate can be abraded off: If only a small area needs to be removed, emery paper or an abrasive wheel on the micromotor will take plate off.
Send for chemical stripping: Completely removing plate can be difficult, because there are frequently hard-to-access areas. In this case it is best to find a company that can strip the piece chemically. The plating company may well be able to do this.

▲ Use a buff stick to abrade the plate off the piece.

Patination

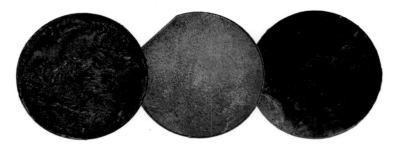

▲ Platinol – scaly and brittle   ▲ Platinol – patchy   ▲ Cupric nitrate – black

THE PROBLEM

Patina has gone scaly, patchy, black or you simply don't like it

THE CAUSES

Scaly and brittle: Too much patina has built up. This happens when the patina builds up too quickly or when the piece has been exposed to the chemicals repeatedly.

Patchy: The piece is not entirely grease-free. Application of solution might have been uneven.

Cupric nitrate has gone black: The piece has been overheated.

Does not suit the piece: You might decide that another colour would be more effective on your design.

THE SOLUTION

Remove the patina and reapply:
- Scrub off excess patina with a stiff brush; scrub with soap and pumice; or heat up with a torch, then quench and pickle.
- Reapply the patina (or a different patina) if required. Rinse well between coats and rub with a soft brush.
- To avoid patchiness, take care not to touch the piece with your fingers. The piece has been properly degreased when water lies on the surface evenly. Try dipping the piece briefly in the solution for even coverage.
- To avoid a build-up of patina, you may need to dilute the oxidising solution.
- For cupric nitrate, take care not to overheat the piece.

▲ Scrub off the patina with a stiff brush.

▲ Or use heat to remove the patina.

THE PROBLEM

Patina keeps flaking off

Caused by: The surface it is being applied to is too shiny and the patina cannot adhere.

▲ Platinol applied to a shiny surface.

THE SOLUTION

Create a key on the surface: Abrade the surface with fairly fine emery paper (800–1000 grit). This should give enough texture for the solution to stick to.

▶ Use a buff stick to sand off the flaking patina and create a key on the surface.

Polishing

THE PROBLEM

After polishing, some of the detail has vanished

Caused by: The piece has been pushed too hard into the mop, resulting in the detail being rubbed off.

THE SOLUTION

Proceed with caution in future: Try to re-create the texture. This may mean returning to the triblet to rehammer a texture, or stopping out and re-etching.

◀ An area of texture has been rubbed off during polishing.

THE PROBLEM

The piece is not as highly polished as it should be

Caused by: The piece might have been coated in too much polishing compound, preventing the mop from doing its job. The mop may be contaminated with a coarser polishing compound.

THE SOLUTIONS

Clean and repolish: Clean the piece with hot water and liquid detergent and repolish using less compound this time.
Wash the mop: If the problem persists, it might be because the mop is contaminated. Try holding a wire brush against the mop as it spins. Mops can be laundered in the washing machine.

▲ Hold a wire brush against the polishing mop to remove contaminants from the mop.

THE PROBLEM

Scratches or a dark shadow have appeared

Caused by: These are the result of earlier processes. Scratches are the result of inadequate finishing prior to polishing. A dark shadow is firestain, caused by the copper in the sterling silver alloy oxidising when heated. It is often only revealed at the polishing stage.

THE SOLUTIONS

Remove the scratches: It is always worth going back to the tripoli stage to see if scratches can be eradicated there. Any really deep marks will have to be dealt with using emery paper.

Grind off the firestain: Firestain can be ground off by a variety of means (see page 67). If abrasive methods are likely to damage the texture of the piece, continue polishing as normal and get the piece silver-plated.

▲ Scratches may only be revealed after polishing.

▲ Firestain often only becomes visible after polishing.

CHAPTER 4

WIREWORK

Although wire is now used for all kinds of electrical and industrial purposes, it was first made to be used in jewellery by the Egyptians in about 2600 BCE. Then, as now, metal would be pulled through small apertures to 'draw' it down. Wire can be used to make all kinds of chains, links and weaves, and it is essential in making mounts for stones; it also has the unique quality of making fluid forms from normally unyielding materials. If handled carelessly, wire pieces can look messy and amateurish, but when properly considered and finished, they can have an elegance and weightlessness that is hard to achieve in any other medium.

Preparing the wire

The starting point for any of the wirework techniques in this chapter involves annealing and straightening the wire. Small lengths of wire can be made straight by rolling them between two flat steel plates, while longer lengths can be straightened by putting one end in a vice and pulling with draw tongs.

▲ KATHARINA VONES
The wire structure enables this brooch to be simultaneously light and strong.

As with sheet metal, alloyed wire needs to be annealed to render it malleable enough to form, as well as to eliminate its inherent springiness. Wire is often sold as half-hard or fully annealed. If you buy a whole reel of such wire, it may remain quite soft. However, if you only buy a length of it, handling and transportation will have caused it to become work-hardened, so it is usually best to anneal it yourself.

Annealing the wire

It is best to wrap the wire into a coil before annealing it. This allows the whole length of the wire to be annealed evenly, which will result in it behaving in the same way all along its length.

Wrap the length of wire into a coil and tuck in the ends neatly (any exposed bits of wire are liable to get hotter than the rest and might melt). This will bend the ends of the wire, but you can simply cut these off if you are working in base metal. If you are using more costly precious metal, wrap the whole coil evenly in binding wire to hold it together. Remember to remove the steel binding wire before pickling.

Heat the wire coil evenly with a torch, making sure that the whole coil reaches annealing temperature. It might be necessary to turn it over halfway through. Wire can also be annealed in a kiln. Coil the wire and place it in an old tin can to keep it together, then put the can into a preheated kiln (800°C/1472°F) for a few minutes. With either method, finish by quenching and pickling.

Drawing down wire

The draw bench is a piece of equipment that is designed for gripping wire and pulling it through holes in a steel draw plate in order to change the diameter/shape of the wire. If you have access to a draw bench, you need only keep one kind of wire in stock. You can then draw it down to the size or shape you need for the piece you are working on. The draw bench is also useful for the final stage of tube making, and for pulling finished chain through to even it up.

Draw benches are quite large and expensive, so most people only have access to one when attending a college course. However, wire can also be pulled through a draw plate manually by fastening it in a vice and pulling the wire through using draw tongs. Draw tongs are heavy-duty pliers with textured grips on the jaws for gripping the wire.

▲ Coil of silver wire wrapped in binding wire, ready for annealing.

▼ Annealing a coil of wire, with the ends neatly tucked in.

WHAT'S THE PROBLEM?

SHAPING

DECORATION

WIREWORK

CASTING

STONE SETTING

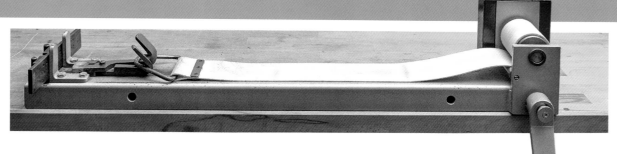

Using a draw bench

1 Make a long point at one end of the annealed wire using a rolling mill or file. The point should be shallow and fine enough to pass through the draw plate on the gauge you finally require.

▲ A draw bench is used to reduce the diameter of wire, to change its shape and to straighten it.

2 Select a hole in the draw plate very slightly finer than the wire, pull the pointed end of the wire through and grip it with the draw tongs. It can be helpful to apply some light oil to the wire waiting to go through the plate, but take care not to get oil on to the tapered tip because this can cause the draw tongs to slip. Alternatively, rub a little beeswax on to the wire.

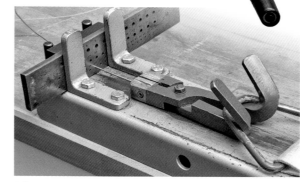

3 Gently turn the handle, trying to turn it evenly. Be aware that the free end of the wire might spring through the plate at the end, so wear goggles. Repeat until you achieve the desired size or shape. You will need to anneal the wire regularly because drawing it down will work-harden it.

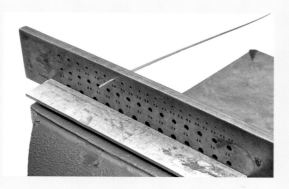

Using a vice

If you do not have access to a draw bench, secure the draw plate in a sturdy vice (always secure it upright in the vice). Grip the end of the wire with draw tongs and pull it through the draw plate manually in a single smooth motion. This usually means walking backwards through the workshop, so make sure the path you will take is clear of obstacles.

Making jump rings

Jump ring is the standard term for a piece of wire that has been bent into a circle. It is one of the primary linking methods in jewellery. Jump rings are generally circular and vary in wire thickness and diameter.

▲ CHRISTINE KALTOFT
Contrasting jump rings connect the wire elements in this neckpiece.

Jump rings are manufactured commercially, but they can easily be made in the workshop. The techniques for making jump rings can also be used for producing batches of band rings or bangles.

Making one or two jump rings

Decide on the thickness of wire required, then anneal and pickle it. If you only need one or two jump rings, use a pair of round-nose pliers and wrap the wire into a spiral on whichever part of the pliers gives you the right size. Remove the spiral from the pliers, hold it flat on the bench peg where the two ends overlap and saw through them. The jump rings usually end up on the saw blade, but put the bench skin over your lap to catch them in case they ping off.

▶ Use round-nose pliers to make just a couple of jump rings.

Making a batch of jump rings

Using a former If you need to make a batch of jump rings all the same size, find a former of the right diameter – the smooth end of a drill bit, a doming punch or chasing tool, or a length of wooden dowel. Aluminium knitting needles also make very good formers – they come in a wide variety

▲ Use a former such as wooden dowel to make a batch of identically sized rings.

of sizes and are easy to obtain. Put the former into a vice, pointing upwards, and trap one end of the wire in with it. Alternatively, if the material permits, you can drill a hole in the former and thread the wire through it. Carefully wind the wire around the former, keeping it neat and tight. Use a piece of wooden dowel or a small soft mallet to tap the links down to keep them as neatly packed as possible.

Using a drill If you are making a serious quantity of jump rings, a mandrel can be inserted into a cordless drill held in a vice. Use the lowest speed to turn the mandrel slowly and guide the wire to keep it neat. A hand drill held in a vice with the handle facing upwards can also be used. Guiding the wire with your hands when using a power tool is not a good idea, so use a piece of cloth or leather wrapped over the wire to prevent injury. A good low-tech guide can be made from a wooden clothes peg. Drill a hole through one of the pincers so that the wire is fed into the groove where the bulk of cloth would fit and out over the lip of the pincer.

WHAT'S THE PROBLEM?

SHAPING

DECORATION

WIREWORK

CASTING

STONE SETTING

Making multiple jump rings using a drill

1 Fit a mandrel into a drill for making large quantities of identical jump rings.

2 Thread the free end of the wire through a hole drilled in a clothes peg.

3 Use the peg to guide the wire around the mandrel to protect your fingers from injury.

Cutting the rings

Take the wire coil to your bench, ready for sawing. It is worth modifying the bench peg to create a small protrusion, so that the end of the coil can be put over this to help keep everything firmly in place and stop the wire from wobbling about too much. Wrapping masking tape around the length of the spring can also help to keep the rings from moving as you try to saw them.

Angle the saw blade at 45 degrees so that it cuts through two pieces of wire at once. It is tempting to reach for the wire cutters at this point, but using a saw for this is infinitely preferable because the ends of the jump rings will fit together perfectly and will not be pinched by the cutters.

◄ Customise your bench peg to create a protrusion for holding the wire coil.

◄ Hold the saw at 45 degrees so that you cut through two jump rings at once.

Opening and closing jump rings

Grip the jump ring using two pairs of flat- or needle-nose pliers, one on either side of the opening. To open the jump ring, push one pair of pliers backwards while pulling the other pair forwards. To close the jump ring, reverse this action and wiggle backwards and forwards until the ends meet perfectly.

▲ Twist the ends of the jump ring backwards and forwards to open and close it. Never pull the ends apart as this will weaken the ring.

Chain making

As with many jewellery techniques, chain making is a vast subject. There are lots of different linking styles, from simple open-link chain to the most complicated Byzantine weave. Be warned – it is very addictive.

◄ SIAN EVANS
Graduated gauge width and link sizes have been put to skilful use in this bracelet.

Chains can be constructed from any components that are capable of being linked. They do not have to be made exclusively from jump rings (and jump rings do not have to be circular), but plain old jump rings can be made to do fabulous things with a bit of ingenuity.

Wire thickness ratio

One of the crucial considerations when embarking on a chain-making project is getting the ratio between the size of the jump ring and the thickness of the wire correct: too large and fine and the chain will be loose and weak; too small and thick and it will be hard to make.

Make a note of the required ratio and apply it to the size of wire that you have available. For example, the ratio for box chain is about 4:1, so 1mm thick wire should be wrapped around a 4mm diameter former to make the jump rings. There is a degree of latitude with most chains, so experiment to see what you like best. When starting a new chain, keep a record of how many jump rings you have and what length of chain they make – this could be useful for future projects.

Basic chain making

The most basic chain construction simply involves linking jump rings together one after the other to make a simple open chain. Make the jump rings of the shape and size you require. A ratio of 2.2:1 makes a fairly chunky chain.

Preparation Divide the jump rings into two groups. With one group, make sure that the cut ends of each jump ring are aligned (hold the ring in two sets of flat- or needle-nose pliers and wiggle the ends back and forth until they meet tightly). Lay this group of jump rings on to a fireproof surface, with the cut ends all facing the same way, ready for soldering. Flux the joints and balance small pallions of solder on them. Heat until the solder melts. Alternatively,

▶ Lay the jump rings on to a fireproof surface, cut ends all facing in the same direction, ready for soldering.

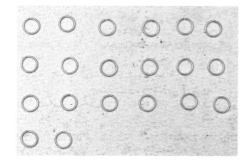

CHAIN TYPE	BOX CHAIN	BYZANTINE	SIMPLE ETRUSCAN	DOUBLE-BACKED ETRUSCAN	DOUBLE-AXIS ETRUSCAN
WIRE THICKNESS	0.8mm sterling silver	0.9mm (no.5 cookson)	0.8mm gilding metal	0.5mm brass	0.6mm fine silver
DOWEL WIDTH	6mm (7.5:1 ratio, but try 4:1)	3.2mm	9.5mm	9.5mm	12mm

WHAT'S THE PROBLEM?

SHAPING

DECORATION

WIREWORK

CASTING

STONE SETTING

use a pick to apply solder. Note: If using fine silver or high-carat gold, the metal can be fused without using solder at all. Just get the ends to meet perfectly and heat until you see a flash around the joint. Quench and pickle, then file or sand off any excess solder.

Joining the links Get one of the open jump rings and slip two of the closed ones on to it. Wiggle it closed using two pairs of pliers, making sure the ends meet perfectly. Hold the two soldered rings together in a pair of reverse-action tweezers (or a third hand), with the unsoldered (but perfectly aligned) ends of the other jump ring facing upwards. Apply flux and solder, and then heat. The pliers will act as a heat sink and protect the previously soldered jump rings from the heat. If you prefer, the solder can be applied with a soldering pick, which prevents it from blowing off. Keep joining three jump rings at a time, then join these together to make a chain.

▲ RALPH BAKKER
Clever internal construction unites this repeated form bracelet.

▲ Use reverse-action pliers to hold jump rings for soldering together.

Finishing off chains

Whether you have made a simple open chain as described above, or one of the more complex constructions overleaf, you will need to neaten the links and true up the chain before polishing it.

Trueing up An upholsterer's needle or a fine knitting needle placed upright in a vice can be used to true up the finished chain. Push each link on to it in turn to make the links more regular. Chain can also be pulled through a large hole in a draw plate to true it up. You can make your own chain-pulling draw plate by drilling holes of various sizes in a piece of hardwood (wood is gentler than a steel draw plate). Check all the links to make sure that none has opened.

Polishing Chain is best polished in a barrel polisher, wrapped around a piece of wire to stop it from getting tangled. If the chain has to be polished on a polishing motor, it should be taped to a piece of wood. Never hold it in the hands because it can easily get wrapped around the fingers – with dire consequences. If you are polishing at the bench with a micromotor or pendant motor, hold the chain tightly over the bench peg and polish it in short lengths.

▲ Hold the chain tightly on the bench peg if using a micromotor for polishing.

▲ Use a needle in a vice to neaten individual links.

▲ Make a wooden draw plate to true up your chains.

▲ Wrap the chain around some wire if using a barrel polisher.

Box chain

Also known as Inca puño, this chain involves folding back pairs of links to create an open weave. If the ratio is right, the jump rings should have enough tensile strength to support the chain without being soldered together. A ratio of about 4:1 works well.

1 Open all the jump rings so they are ready to be linked together. Group the links in pairs and link three sets of pairs together. Fasten a length of wire around the first pair of jump rings to mark the end and give you something to hold on to.

2 Separate the final pair of jump rings and push them backwards to expose the pair below.

3 Separate this pair of jump rings to expose the pair that you just pushed backwards, then hook a new pair of jump rings around the exposed pair. Then add another pair to the two you just added.

4 Repeat this process (steps 2–3) until the chain is finished.

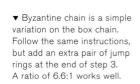

▼ Byzantine chain is a simple variation on the box chain. Follow the same instructions, but add an extra pair of jump rings at the end of step 3. A ratio of 6.6:1 works well.

Chainmail

This classic chainmail weave – the kind worn under suits of armour – is called European 4-in-1. One method of making chainmail is described here, but there are lots of websites devoted to the subject, many of which provide free patterns and tutorials for this and many other weaves. A ratio of 4:1 is used here.

1 Close four jump rings and put them on to an open one. Lay them on the table so that the centre ring has two rings sitting above it and two below. The pair to the left of the centre ring should be resting on top of the other two.

2 Close two more jump rings and put them on to an open one, then pass the ends of the open ring through the left-hand edge of the two links sitting to the left of the centre ring. Continue doing this until you have created the desired width.

3 To build up the next row, rotate the piece 180 degrees so that the central links are pointing to the right. Put two closed rings on to one open ring, and then hook the end through the two links on the bottom left of the first row.

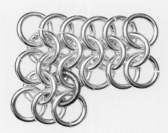

4 From now onwards, put one ring on to an open ring. Pass the open ring through the next ring along on the previous row plus through the one to the left of it, and also through the bottom right one that you added in the previous step.

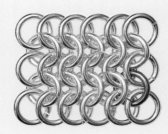

5 Repeat this process until you reach the end of the row. Continue adding rows as required.

WHAT'S THE PROBLEM?

SHAPING

DECORATION

WIREWORK

CASTING

STONE SETTING

Simple Etruscan chain

Also known as Roman or loop-in-loop chain, this ancient chain-making technique results in a complex rope-like chain. Simple Etruscan chain is quite open in appearance, but as links are doubled back, or as an extra axis is added, the chain becomes more dense and snake-like.

1 A ratio of 16.6:1 works well. Solder the links, or fuse if using fine silver. Put a pair of round-nose pliers into each link and open the pliers to pull the link into a rounded rectangle shape.

Double-backed Etruscan chain

Also known as a foxtail chain, this is a denser chain than simple Etruscan. Elongate the links and join the first two links together as before. Now push the top link downwards so that the next one can be woven through the rounded ends of two links instead of one. Repeat this process, always joining one link through the two below it.

2 Bend the links over until the two rounded ends nearly meet. Do this with all the links.

3 Construct the chain by weaving each new link through the rounded ends of the previous link, so that the bent middle section is trapped. The rounded ends can be opened slightly with a scribe or bradawl to make it easier to add the next link and to even up the weave.

4 Once finished, insert a bradawl or scribe through each link from all directions to true up the chain. This makes the chain slightly fatter and shorter. After that, if you wish, you can pull the chain through a draw plate or a hole drilled in a piece of hardwood to even up the weave (this will stretch the chain and elongate the links). Lubricate the chain with beeswax before pulling it through.

Double-axis Etruscan chain

This technique adds another level of density and complexity to the previous Etruscan chains. It works best using fine silver, because it is soft and stretchy and can be fused rather than being soldered. A ratio of 18:1 works well.

1 Elongate the links as before. Without bending them up, solder the bottom two links one on top of the other, at 90 degrees to each other, to form a cross. To make the chain more manageable, these links can either be soldered to a piece of rod, or you can pass a length of wire through them to act as a handle.

2 Bend the links up and open out the rounded ends with a scribe or bradawl.

3 Weave the links together as before, inserting one across one axis and then another across the other axis. You can insert each link through a single link below, or through two links for a double weave. Pull it through a former when finished. Always be on the look out for any fused joints that have failed.

Knitting and crochet

Although it is harder to work than yarn, fine wire can be knitted, crocheted or woven with a French knitting bobbin. The wire has to be quite fine – thinner than 24 gauge (0.5mm). Beads, sequins or any object capable of being threaded can be added.

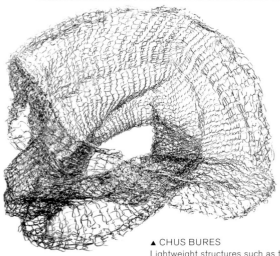

▲ CHUS BURES
Lightweight structures such as this head adornment can be crocheted from fine wire.

The effect is much more open than textile knitting because the stitches cannot be pulled as tightly together. For this reason, there is no point in knitting or crocheting different stitches because the effect would be lost. Fine silver is much easier to work than sterling silver because it is more stretchy and malleable. A cheaper alternative is craft wire, which is made of copper with a coloured coating and comes in a huge variety of colours. If using beads, thread them on to the wire in advance. They can be held in place with tape until needed. To calculate how many beads will be needed, make a sample piece about 2.5cm (1in) square and multiply up to the size of the finished piece. Allow a bit of extra plain wire at the end in case the spacing has to be modified. If you run out of wire, leave a long tail with both ends and weave them into the work in opposite directions when the piece is finished.

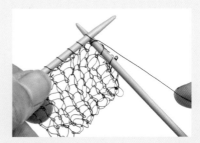

Knitting

A pair of 2.5–3.5mm knitting needles works well. It is also easier to work with short needles. Cast on the required number of stitches, work each row in knit stitch and cast off as you would with yarn.

Crochet

A 4mm hook works well. Make the required number of foundation chains and then work in double crochet stitch throughout. Take care not to pull the wire too tightly.

French knitting

French knitting bobbins can be found in toy shops, or you can make your own with headless nails or wire loops hammered around the central hole of an old thread reel. They can have four, six or eight pegs.

WHAT'S THE PROBLEM?

SHAPING

DECORATION

WIREWORK

CASTING

STONE SETTING

Twisting wire

The world of wirework takes another twist. Twisted fine wires are used in filigree work and can add interest to stone settings; thicker ones make great bangles or torques.

▼ ELIZAVETA GNATCHENKO
Wire is used to create playful flowing lines in this neckpiece.

Square or triangular wire can be twisted singly to great effect. Round wires can be doubled over to create a twine effect. Metals can be mixed, as can the gauges and profiles, leading to numerous variations.

▶ Use an eyebolt and drill held in a vice to twist doubled wire.

Twisting single wire

The best results when twisting a single wire are obtained by using cross-sectional shapes with edges – round wires do not change at all when twisted. Anneal the wire and secure one end in a vice. Hold the end with a pair of draw tongs, a ring clamp or pliers, then pull taut and twist.

It is possible just to twist certain sections of the wire by controlling which parts are held in the vice and which are twisted. The sections can be twisted in opposite directions to great effect. Remember to count the number of twists to make sure that both sections match.

Twisting doubled or multiple wires

Always work with annealed wire. To twist a doubled wire, feed the wire through a hook or eyebolt set into a hand or electric drill and fix the two ends in a vice. Pull the wire taut, and turn the drill until the wire is twisted. It is best to overtwist slightly because it will unwind a bit when released.

If using two or three different types of wire, knot them together at one end (or solder them all together). Hold this end in a vice. Cut the other ends so that they are all even, and insert them into the jaws of the drill, clamp or pliers. Pull the wires taut and twist. This wire can then be doubled over on itself and twisted again to form a more rope-like weave. Alternatively, one of the wires can be unwound, leaving the other one in an open spiral form.

The twisted wire can also be annealed and pulled through a draw plate to change the profile of the piece. To do this, solder the end together and hammer or file it into a point, before pulling through the selected hole in the draw plate a few times. Twisted wire can also be flattened by hammering it or passing it through a rolling mill.

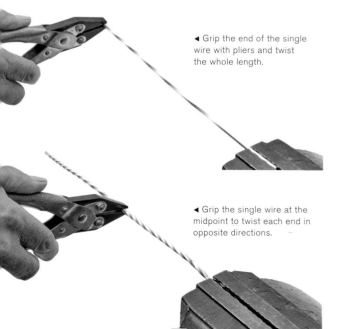

◀ Grip the end of the single wire with pliers and twist the whole length.

◀ Grip the single wire at the midpoint to twist each end in opposite directions.

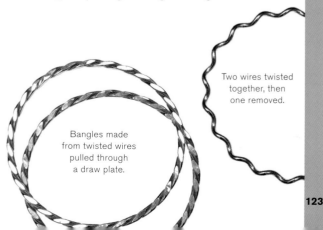

Bangles made from twisted wires pulled through a draw plate.

Two wires twisted together, then one removed.

Making simple findings

Findings is the name given to closing mechanisms, brooch backs, earhooks or any extra piece that is used to finish an item of jewellery and make it fit for purpose.

◄ SHIMARA CARLOW
The earwires in these wrapped wire earrings are integral to the design.

Toggle clasp

Use wire of at least 18 gauge (1mm). The length of the bar should be at least twice the inner diameter of the loop.

1 Make a circle that will form the loop through which the toggle passes. Solder the loop shut, then make it perfectly circular on a small mandrel. Cut a length of wire for the bar, about 13mm (½in), and straighten it between two flat steel plates.

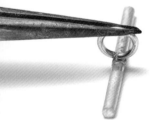

2 Locate the centre point of the bar and file a groove into it with a round needle file. Solder a jump ring into this groove. Place it so that the joint in the ring is soldered shut when attached to the straight wire.

3 Attach the loop and the toggle to the piece of jewellery. If the toggle is too long to fit through the loop, file the ends down evenly and keep checking it. The toggle must fit through the loop but should be as long as possible to prevent it from falling off.

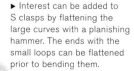

► Interest can be added to S clasps by flattening the large curves with a planishing hammer. The ends with the small loops can be flattened prior to bending them.

S clasp

Decide how heavy the clasp should be – better that it is slightly too heavy than too flimsy. Estimate how much wire it will need by drawing the clasp on paper and bending scrap wire to fit the drawing. Straighten it out and measure it.

1 If necessary, straighten the piece of wire by putting it between two steel plates and rolling it backwards and forwards. Finish both ends of the wire nicely, either rounded or filed flat. Bend each end into a small loop, using the very tip of some round-nose pliers. The loops should face in opposite directions.

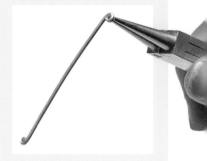

2 Bend the large curves of the S shape, making sure that the tiny loops at the ends are facing outwards.

3 Using half-round pliers, spend a little time making sure that the curves are identical.

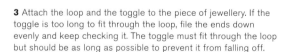

Ear posts

Ear posts are usually made of 19–20 gauge wire (0.8 to 0.9mm). They are around 11mm (⅜in) long.

1 If necessary, anneal and straighten the wire by rolling it between two steel plates. Cut the ear posts to size.

2 File them so that one end is perfectly flat and the end that will go through the ear is nicely rounded without a point. This can be achieved easily with a cup burr.

3 Solder the post to the back of the earring. After soldering, the post will be too soft because it will have annealed.

4 Posts can be work-hardened in several ways. Barrel polishing is the easiest method. You can also burnish the post until it is hard, or grip it firmly in flat-faced pliers and twist several times (this is a good test for the strength of the solder joint).

5 If you want a little groove for the butterfly to sit in, hold the ear post in a pair of end cutters. Close the cutters and apply very slight pressure while twisting the earring and post around.

Ear hooks

Ear hooks can take many different forms. Try drawing different shapes to see which works best for the piece. Make a rough version in binding wire first to see how much wire you should cut. Cut two pieces of wire to the same length and finish the ends nicely, paying particular attention to the end that will go through the ear, which should be rounded without a point.

1 Make a small loop at one end of the wire with round-nose pliers. Use the pliers to put a slight bend at the other end of the wire.

2 Bend the hook over with the pliers. It might be necessary to adjust the shape of the curve slightly with half-round pliers.

◀ In its simplest form, an ear hook is half an S clasp.

▼ For long ear hooks that are soldered directly on to the earring, bend the end that will go through the ear slightly with pliers, then bend the hook around a suitable former, such as a mandrel, to achieve the required curve.

WHAT'S THE PROBLEM?

SHAPING

DECORATION

WIREWORK

CASTING

STONE SETTING

THE PROBLEM

Metal is moving through the plate very jerkily

Caused by: Metal needs to be re-annealed or lubricated.

THE SOLUTIONS

Re-anneal: Roll the wire up into a neat coil and anneal.

Lubricate: Lubricate the wire behind the draw plate. Rub a little beeswax or candle wax on it or put a little oil on to a cloth and pull it along the length of the wire. Be careful not to get it on the pointy part or it will be impossible to grip. Turn the handle of the draw plate as smoothly as possible.

▲ Lubricate the wire with beeswax.

THE PROBLEM

I need to make a piece of wire that is longer than the draw bench

Caused by: This often happens if you are drawing a piece of fairly thick wire down to a very fine gauge.

THE SOLUTIONS

Pull the wire manually: If the room you are working in allows, release the draw tongs from the bench and walk backwards at a steady rate, pulling the wire manually. Use parallel pliers to pull very thin wire through.

Move the tongs closer: If this is not possible, reattach the draw tongs close to where the wire is emerging from the plate and then continue. The tongs may mark this section of wire, but this can be sanded or cut off later.

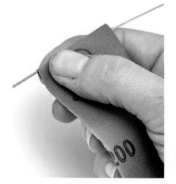

▲ Use emery paper to sand off any marks left by the tongs where they were reattached.

THE PROBLEM

The tongs cannot grip the metal firmly enough and keep slipping off

Caused by: The point of the wire is not protruding far enough through the hole. Oil or some other lubricant is on the tongs or on the end of the metal.

THE SOLUTIONS

Taper the wire more: File down the wire more, keeping the taper very long. Make sure you get the end of the tongs right up to the draw plate.

Clean the wire and tongs: Wipe the end of the metal and the tongs to make sure they are not slippery.

▶ The point of the wire should protrude by about 1cm (³⁄₈in).

▲ The point of the wire is not protruding enough.

WHAT'S THE PROBLEM?

SHAPING

DECORATION

WIREWORK

CASTING

STONE SETTING

fix-
its

Making jump rings

THE PROBLEM

The jump ring isn't round

Caused by: The wire has not been wrapped tightly enough around the former, or is under-annealed. The rings may not have been parallel and neatly packed together when being wound. The rings may not have been sawn through at a 90-degree angle.

▲ Misshapen jump ring

THE SOLUTIONS

Anneal and wrap tightly: Make sure the wire is annealed properly and wrapped really tightly around the former. If using pliers as a former, make sure the ends of the wire are spiralled past each other.

Hold steady when cutting: If only one or two jump rings are being made, they can be held steady with parallel pliers to keep the saw cut straight.

▲ Always wrap the ends of the wire past each other when forming.

Flatten and file: If you have some wonky jump rings, get the ends to meet as best you can, place them flat on a steel plate, tap them flat with a soft mallet and then file the edges together until they meet nicely. However, it may be quicker to make some new jump rings.

▲ Use a mallet to flatten wonky jump rings.

THE PROBLEM

Jump ring is the wrong size

Caused by: The wire has not been placed on the right part of the round-nose pliers or has not been properly annealed before being wrapped around a former.

THE SOLUTIONS

Measure the pliers: Use a vernier to measure the correct point on the pliers to achieve the inside diameter you require. Mark it with a permanent pen.

Anneal well: Make sure wire is annealed before wrapping a lot of jump rings.

◄ Measure and mark on the pliers the required diameter for the jump rings.

THE PROBLEM

The coil of wire is really hard to hold together when sawing and the jump rings end up looking a bit mangled

Caused by: Because it has become work-hardened when wrapped around the former, the coil of wire is springy. If it is quite long, it can bend in the hand and be hard to control. If the saw blade or the coil slips, the blade may mark the rings.

▲ Ridges on jump ring caused by the saw blade slipping.

THE SOLUTIONS

Hold steady with parallel pliers: If you are just making one or two jump rings, hold them still with parallel pliers.

Use wooden dowel as a former: If many jump rings are required, use a wooden dowel as a former that can be sawn into.

Modify the bench peg: Alternatively, modify the bench peg so that it has a piece protruding from it that the coil can rest against while it is being sawn.

Tape before sawing: Wrap masking tape around the spring to hold it together and to help prevent the saw blade from slipping. With practice, you will evolve an efficient way of dealing with this that suits you.

▲ Use parallel pliers to hold the wire steady when sawing.

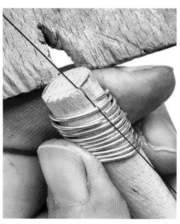

▲ Use wooden dowel as a former and saw into it when cutting the jump rings.

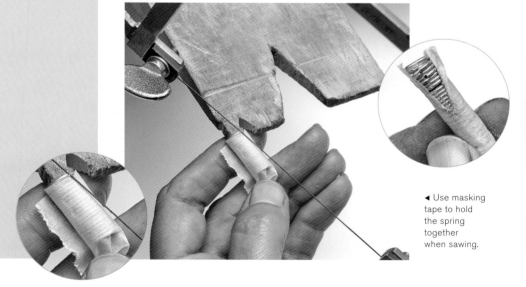

◄ Use masking tape to hold the spring together when sawing.

fix-its

Chain making

THE PROBLEM

Solder keeps blowing off the jump rings when trying to solder them together

Caused by: The draft caused by the gas can easily blow the pieces of solder off.

THE SOLUTIONS

Flux well: When cutting the pallions of solder, drop them straight into the flux dish so that they get a good coating. This will help them to stick.

Put the rings on top: Rest the open ends of the jump rings on top of the pallions of solder instead of the other way round.

Use a soldering pick: Melt each pallion of solder on the end of a soldering pick and apply it to the hot fluxed joint (it takes practice to perfect this, but is worth the effort).

▶ Put the jump ring on top of the solder.

THE PROBLEM

Fine silver keeps melting rather than fusing

Caused by: Too much heat has been applied.

THE SOLUTIONS

Space them out: Leave more space between the rings when laying them on the soldering block.

Look for the flash: Move the torch as soon as you see a little flash on the jump ring, which indicates that the metal has melted. Work in an area that is not too brightly lit so that this can be observed.

◀ Melted rings

▲ Space out the rings on the soldering block.

THE PROBLEM

Solder keeps going in the wrong place when constructing the chain

Caused by: Solder will run to the hottest area, or will follow the flux.

THE SOLUTIONS

Be accurate: Use a tiny brush to apply the flux and very small pallions of solder.

Position the links carefully: Take time when arranging the chain on the reverse-action tweezers. You can make the most of the fact that the steel acts as a heat sink by positioning the links so that the two that are already soldered will be protected by the tweezers.

Liquefy the solder: If the links have become soldered together, reheat them gently until the solder liquefies, then keep the links in motion while the torch is taken away and the metal cools. If that fails, the soldered links will have to be removed from the chain.

▲ Use tweezers to protect rings that have already been soldered from the heat.

THE PROBLEM

Issues with ratio of wire thickness to circle size – too spindly and weak; too heavy to get links through

Caused by: Particularly when trying out different linking systems, it can take some experimentation to get the ratio of wire thickness to internal diameter right.

THE SOLUTIONS

Make a test piece: Only make enough jump rings to make a test piece of 2.5–5cm (1–2in) to start with. Be critical with this and check that it fills the criteria you defined at the start of the project. Make a note of the wire gauge and former width used.

Double-check instructions: If you are following chain-making instructions that have been published in a book and have problems with the ratio, check very carefully that you are following the instructions properly.

◄ This piece is almost too open to work as a functioning bracelet.

THE PROBLEM

There is a mistake in the chain weave or you have lost your place in the weave

Caused by: Often when reviewing a chain, you will notice a mistake quite near the start – this has happened when you were getting into the rhythm of the chain and learning the weave. Losing your place in the weave can sometimes be due to a simple lapse in concentration or the phone ringing. Making a chain with large open links can be more confusing than using smaller, tighter ones.

THE SOLUTIONS

Unpick up to the error: If the error is near the start of the chain, continue until you have reached the length you need. Mark the first link that is correct after the mistake, either with a piece of wire or by marking it with a permanent pen, and then unpick the chain from the start point up to the marked link. Then use the resulting jump rings to finish the chain. You might need to re-anneal and pickle them if they have become too work-hardened.

Unpick back to the error: If you notice the error fairly promptly, just unpick the chain until you are at a stage before the mistake.

Find your place again: If you have lost your place in the weave, turn the chain 90 degrees – sometimes it looks wrong because it is at the wrong angle. Unpicking a couple of links often helps to find the place.

Mark your place: If you have to stop for any reason, wind a piece of wire around the next link to be joined so that it will be easy to pick up where you left off.

◄ Mark the first link after the error, then unpick from the start end up to the marked link.

THE PROBLEM

Completed chain is uneven or unfinished

Caused by: Chain needs to be trued up.

▲ Uneven chain

THE SOLUTIONS

True up each link: If the chain is fairly open (such as Etruscan chain), the links can be made even and round by fastening a narrow knitting needle or scribe upright in a vice and pushing each link on to it.

Use a draw plate: Chain can also be pulled through a hole drilled in a piece of wood, or through a large hole in a draw plate, to make it more regular. Always check that no soldered joints have failed after drawing it.

▲ True up each link on a scribe fixed upright in a vice.

THE PROBLEM

A fine silver link has snapped

Caused by: Some links are weaker than others, either due to too much heat being applied that has partially melted the chain, or insufficient heat to make a strong joint.

THE SOLUTIONS

Check the links:
■ Before starting the chain, look at every link and reject any failures.
■ Make a pile of the perfect ones and another pile of any you are unsure of. Start the chain with the unsure pile. If any are going to fail, it is better that they go at the start end of the chain, which is often not as beautiful as the finish end, which will be made when you have perfected the rhythm.

▲ If you hear or notice a link failing while you are making the chain, go back and remove it.

THE PROBLEM

Chain has got all tangled up in the barrel polisher

Caused by: Short pieces of chain can be barrelled on their own with no problem, but if you have more than one chain, or if they are quite long, they can get tangled.

◄ Tangled chain

THE SOLUTIONS

Wrap with wire: Prevent tangling by attaching a piece of wire to one end. Wrap the chain around the wire, and then wrap the end of the wire back around the chain.

Tease the links apart: Set the chain flat on a table and gently waggle it to tease apart the tangles. Find one end and gradually release it from its knots. For fine chain, use two scribes or pieces of wire to help in the waggling process.

▲ Use two scribes to help tease apart the tangles.

WHAT'S THE PROBLEM?

SHAPING

DECORATION

WIREWORK

CASTING

STONE SETTING

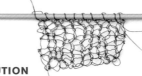

THE PROBLEM

Wire has snapped

Caused by: You may be pulling the wire too tightly or the wire may be too fine. It is more difficult if you are using sterling silver, which is not as ductile as fine silver.

THE SOLUTION

Join in a new length of wire: Undo a few stitches to leave a long tail, then introduce a new length of annealed wire, also leaving a tail. Carry on, taking care not to pull the wire too tightly. Once finished, the tail ends can be woven into the piece in opposite directions to hide them when finished.

Weave the tails of wire into the piece afterwards to secure the ends.

THE PROBLEM

Wire has developed a kink

Caused by: This sometimes happens as the wire is unravelled from the reel.

THE SOLUTION

Straighten it out: Flatten the kink in the jaws of a set of flat-nose pliers, or run a burnisher down it.

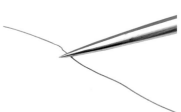

▲ Use flat-nose pliers to straighten out kinks in the wire.

▲ Run a burnisher along the wire to straighten it.

THE PROBLEM

Dropped stitches in French knitting

Caused by: Sometimes a stitch can fall off the dolly without your noticing until you get back to that peg.

THE SOLUTION

Unpick back to the error: Stop as soon as you realise the stitch has dropped. Carefully unpick the work as far as the dropped stitch, and then pick up the dropped stitch and continue.

▲ Unpick back to the error, then pick up the dropped stitch and continue.

fix-its

Twisting wire

THE PROBLEM

Wires are unravelling as soon as they are twisted

Caused by: The wire has been under-annealed. Even annealed wire will twist back slightly because the twisting process will work-harden it.

THE SOLUTION

Undo and start again: Unravel the wires, coil neatly, anneal and pickle, then re-twist.

▲ Unravel the wires completely.

▲ Wrap into a coil and anneal.

▲ Pickle and then retwist.

THE PROBLEM

Wire has got into a knot in the middle or snapped when being twisted

Caused by: Wire that gets into a knot may have been overwound, or the wire was not held taut when twisting it. Snapped wire may not have been annealed enough, or might have become weak from being over-annealed.

THE SOLUTIONS

Untwist knotted wire and start again: Hold the wire taut and unwind it; the central knotted part should unwind as you do so. Hold it straight and taut again, and then rewind it.

Twist each snapped section: Fortunately, wires usually break near the ends when they have reached the maximum they can be twisted to. If wire breaks in the middle, it might be possible to carry on winding the broken end that is still in the vice. The other half may also be returned to the vice and twisted (they might need to be re-annealed if they refuse to twist nicely).

▲ A knot is caused by over-winding the wire or not holding it taut.

THE PROBLEM

Wire has been twisted, but appears the same

Caused by: Only wire with edges will show the twist (that is, square or triangular wire). Round or oval wire does not change.

THE SOLUTION

Use more than one wire: If you want to twist round wire, two wires must be twisted together, like rope or yarn.

▲ Two colours of round wire twisted together.

▲ Use wire with edges, such as square or triangular, if only twisting one wire.

Making simple findings

THE PROBLEM

Spirals on S clasp are incorrect, the clasp won't fasten or just comes apart

THE CAUSES

Wrongly aligned spirals: Because the small spirals are bent up first, it is easy to get them back to front until you get familiar with the technique.

Clasp won't fasten: The spirals are too large to fit through the jump ring.

Clasp pulls apart: The wire of the clasp may be too flimsy, or the bracelet may be a bit tight.

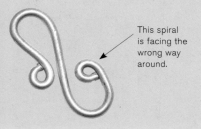

This spiral is facing the wrong way around.

THE SOLUTIONS

Spirals wrong way round:
■ Anneal the hook. Using parallel pliers, grip the small spiral gently and twist it around until it faces the right way.

Clasp won't fasten:
■ It is best to check that the clasp will work before assembling the piece of jewellery. Try compressing the spiral with a pair of straight pliers, or re-wind it using the very tip of round-nose pliers.
■ It may be necessary to make a larger jump ring for the fastening or to remake the S clasp.

Clasp pulls apart:
■ Remake the S clasp in thicker gauge wire. It will be stronger if it is soldered on to the bracelet (it must be work-hardened after soldering with a burnisher or in a barrel polisher).
■ Add a couple of links to the bracelet to ensure it is generous enough.

▲ Use parallel pliers to twist a wrongly positioned spiral round the right way.

▲ To make a spiral smaller, rewind it using round-nose pliers.

THE PROBLEM

Can't fit earring back on to post

Caused by: Sometimes commercially produced butterflies are quite tight.

THE SOLUTION

Open up the butterfly: If you have made the ear post from 0.8 or 0.9mm wire, the discrepancy should be minimal. Try placing both thumbnails through the gap where the scrolls meet. This should separate them enough to allow the wire to pass through.
Enlarge the hole: If that does not work, the hole may be too tight, so enlarge it slightly with a broacher or a 0.9mm drill bit in a pin vice.

▲ Push your thumbnails between the scrolls to loosen them slightly.

WHAT'S THE PROBLEM?

SHAPING

DECORATION

WIREWORK

CASTING

STONE SETTING

THE PROBLEM

Toggle clasp won't fasten or keeps coming undone

THE CAUSES

Comes undone: If the bracelet is slightly too large, it is easy for the toggle to undo itself even if the clasp itself is fine.

Won't fasten: Before attaching to the jewellery, this type of clasp can look like it will not work. If it really doesn't, the jump ring on the bar may be too large or the bar itself too long.

THE SOLUTIONS

Keeps coming undone:
■ Make the bracelet slightly shorter. It should fit snugly on the wrist when fastened; this very slight tension is what keeps it shut.
■ For extra security, a short length of safety chain can be attached to each side of the opening with jump rings.

Won't fasten:
■ Attach the clasp to the piece and try again. The extra wiggle room created by the piece being articulated usually allows the bar to pass through with ease.
■ If it still will not work, you may have used a jump ring that was too large on the bar and this is preventing it from passing through the loop, in which case replace it with a smaller ring, or it might be necessary to file down the length of the bar.

◀ Add a safety chain to a loose-fitting bracelet.

▼ Jump ring on toggle is too large.

THE PROBLEM

The earrings don't dangle properly on the hooks

Caused by: The balance may be slightly off once the weight of the earring is on the hook.

THE SOLUTIONS

Adjust the hoop: Slightly change the curve of the ear hook with half-round pliers, or try using a larger or smaller former to alter the hoop.
Add jump rings for more movement: If the earrings are not moving enough, add two jump rings to the small loop at the front.

▲ Use a former to adjust the size of the hoop.

▶ Add jump rings to give more movement to the earrings.

CHAPTER 5

CASTING

Like so many jewellery processes, casting is an ancient art – the earliest cast objects discovered are more than 5,700 years old. The obvious advantage of casting from moulds is that identical objects can be made, either as pieces of finished jewellery or as elements of a larger item. Casting also has economic advantages – there is little waste as metal can constantly be recycled and reused. The initial labour in making the master and mould for a cast piece is a one-off expense, offset by the potential income from a successful piece.

Casting techniques

Lost wax casting is an ancient technique that involves making a wax model that is then cast in metal. The wax model is burned away in the process, hence the name. Cuttlefish casting uses the soft bone found in cuttlefish to create metal casts.

▲ FRIEDA MUNRO These rings were cast using the lost wax casting technique.

▲ Silver lost wax castings attached by sprues to the tree.

Lost wax casting

Generally in the jewellery business, lost wax casting is a service performed by highly skilled craftspeople using specialised equipment. The wax model supplied by the jeweller can either be carved using files and hand tools, or it can be produced from a mould (see page 142). Waxes can also be created by rapid prototyping machines.

The caster attaches all of the waxes to be cast on to a conical piece of wax known as a tree. The wax models are attached to the tree with sprues, which are little rods made of wax. A skilled caster will know the best way to attach these objects and the correct order in which they should be positioned. Once the tree has been built, it is placed upside down in a flask, with the base of the trunk facing the top. The flask is then filled with a special type of plaster called investment plaster. Once the plaster has hardened, the flask is placed in a kiln and heated to burn out the wax (jeweller's wax burns away at a fairly low temperature, leaving no residue). This results in a plaster mould that is now ready to accept molten metal.

The metal is heated to the optimum temperature for casting and poured into the plaster mould. Successful casting depends on a thorough knowledge of flow dynamics – the caster has to know how best to get the molten metal to flow into the mould so that it fills all the spaces. Historically, centrifugal force was applied to make sure that the metal reached the farthest part of the mould. This used to mean swinging the flask on a chain as soon as the metal was poured. Modern casting machines have a vacuum chamber that ensures all the metal is sucked into the mould in a rather undramatic way.

The flask is then quenched in cold water, the plaster falls away and the metal tree with all the cast elements is revealed. The pieces of jewellery are then cut off the tree; the caster will reuse the metal that forms the tree for the next casting. The resulting pieces of jewellery will have a small piece of sprue left on them that has to be taken off in the workshop.

Carving wax

Jeweller's carving wax comes in several different grades of hardness. Blue is relatively soft and malleable, green is quite hard and brittle, and red is more or less like chewing gum. The wax comes in various different forms – blocks, cylinders, various ring shapes, slabs,

▲ Ring blank wax and reamer

WHAT'S THE PROBLEM?

SHAPING

DECORATION

WIREWORK

CASTING

STONE SETTING

▼ Wax blade

thin sheets and wires – and this can save lots of time when making a wax model. When using a ready-cut ring blank shape, the ring size can be increased by twisting a reamer (a triblet with a blade in it) through the hole to increase the ring size.

▲ Twist the reamer into the hole of the ring blank wax to increase the ring size.

Wax carving tools Wax is best sawn with special wax blades. These are piercing blades that have a spiral construction; normal piercing blades tend to get clogged up with wax very quickly. Wax can be carved with picks and specialised wax carving tools. Dental tools also make very good wax carving tools but can be quite expensive. Burrs on a micromotor or pendant motor work well – keep the speed low so as not to melt the wax.

Heated pens are available for carving wax, or carving tools heated with a paraffin lamp can be used. An electrical soldering iron is another very useful tool when working with wax; you can modify the tips to achieve different uses.

Wax carving files are rougher than metal files and remove lots of wax very efficiently; they don't clog up like metalworking files would. The surface of wax can be refined with fine wire wool, or it can be briefly (and carefully) passed through a flame to smooth it. When you supply a casting company with a wax, they will decide how best to sprue it up on the casting tree.

Carving a wax model

Make a scale drawing of the piece you intend to make. It is a good idea to sketch it from the front, the side and the top, so that you have an idea of how it will work in three dimensions. Cut the wax to the dimensions of your piece, adding an extra millimetre, then mark out and carve the final form. Wax is much lighter than metal, so you should consider the weight (and cost) of the final object. Solid shapes can be hollowed out with burrs to lighten them. Rub with wire wool to finish. For a fine finish, cut a piece from a pair of tights and use it to rub on a little baby oil. The oil slightly melts the surface of the wax, so wash it off when done.

1 Use dividers to mark the centre points on a wax ring blank.

2 Mark out the overall shape of the ring.

3 Mark out the top of the ring.

4 Use a special wax blade to cut out the main shape.

5 Use a wax file to start refining the shape.

6 Use dividers to mark the midpoint all around.

7 Round off the edges symmetrically.

8 Use a burr to hollow out the inside and make the ring lighter.

Cuttlefish casting

Cuttlefish bone is easy to saw and carve, and original objects can be pushed into it with the hands. Cuttlefish bone can withstand high temperatures, so it is good for making objects in pewter or silver. Cuttlefish casting is not good for finely detailed work. Objects cast in this way have distinctive small ridges on them from the structure of the material.

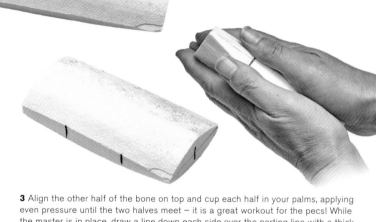

▲ SIAN EVANS
Cuttlefish casting of an antique pilgrim's ring.

Making a cuttlefish mould

1 Choose a nice fat cuttlefish bone. Trim a couple of centimetres off the ends with a piercing saw or a band saw, then saw it down the middle. Cutting off the ends makes it easy to hold it flat and steady when doing this. Rub both sawn surfaces in a circular motion on a piece of emery attached to a flat surface until they fit together perfectly (wear a mask when doing this because it gets dusty). Any gaps will result in flashing when cast.

2 Choose an object to cast that has no undercuts – it must be easy to press into the bone and to lift out. Press the object into the exposed cuttlefish bone about 2.5cm (1in) from the top edge, keeping it straight.

3 Align the other half of the bone on top and cup each half in your palms, applying even pressure until the two halves meet – it is a great workout for the pecs! While the master is in place, draw a line down each side over the parting line with a thick marker; this will help you to align it perfectly later. Short pieces of rod can also be pushed into the cuttlefish when pushing the master in to help with alignment.

4 Open up the cuttlefish mould and extract the master carefully. Cut a funnel-shaped channel from the end of the object to the end of the bone on both sides. This is the pouring gate where the molten metal will be poured. It should be thicker than the thickest part of the object and should be the last part of the casting to cool. Make sure the part where it joins the object being cast is not too narrow.

5 At the pouring gate end of the object, cut a couple of smaller channels running upwards in the same direction as the pouring gate, but only extending for 13mm (½in). These are vents that will allow excess gases and metal to escape. They only need to be made on one side of the mould.

6 Remove any excess dust with a soft brush and reassemble the mould. Hold it together with binding wire, taking care that the registration marks remain in line.

Making a metal cast using cuttlefish

1 Set the cuttlefish mould in a metal bucket, a baking tray full of sand or other secure support, with the sprue hole facing upwards. Heat the metal and pour carefully into the hole. It is worth practising the movement between the hearth or smelter with an empty crucible in the tongs, just to make sure the objects are at the right height and that there is enough room to carry out the operation smoothly and efficiently (it can get a bit too exciting when it comes to pouring molten metal).

2 Allow the metal to solidify for a few minutes. Wearing gloves, snip off the binding wires and pry the two halves apart gently with a knife.

3 The finished piece should come out easily. Quench it in cold water and then clean up the casting.

Cleaning up castings

All castings need to be cleaned up. If using a casting company, different companies treat their castings in different ways before returning them to the customer. Some blast them with a bead blaster, which removes any investment plaster and provides a uniform finish. This can make silver castings appear very grey. Others might give the castings a quick tumble in a barrel polisher. Some might just return it as it comes off the tree after pickling.

The most obvious element to deal with is the sprue. Casting companies usually cut off the sprue quite near the object. The resulting stump can then be filed back or taken back using a rubber wheel on a micromotor. Abrasives or burrs might need to be used to create a texture similar to that around the sprue to disguise its existence.

If you have used a mould for the wax model, check the piece for casting lines that might have happened when wax has escaped through the place where the mould was cut. These can be filed or sanded off, and then any texture can be restored to the piece.

Examine the piece closely and check that there are no tiny pinholes on the surface. Known as porosity, this can be caused if the molten metal is overheated during the casting process. If the piece has a great many holes, it should be returned to the caster because the holes could be throughout the structure of the object, making it brittle. A single pit can be filled with a small piece of wire and some solder, then filed and sanded back. The piece can then be polished in the usual way.

▲ Use a saw blade to cut off the remainder of the sprue if necessary.

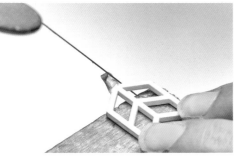

▲ File back the resulting stump.

WHAT'S THE PROBLEM?

SHAPING

DECORATION

WIREWORK

CASTING

STONE SETTING

Mould making

There are two main methods of making moulds for lost wax casting. One is a cold mould made from silicone rubber; the other is a vulcanised mould in which rubber is exposed to heat and pressure to create a sturdy reusable mould.

▲ HENRIETTE LOFSTROM
Taking the time to make a perfect casting master results in beautiful repeated forms, as in these stalactite rings.

Silicone moulds

Silicone moulds are very useful for materials that would be too soft or delicate to tolerate the pressure generated by a vulcaniser. They do not require any specialised equipment. Look at the object you wish to cast and decide which way up it should be positioned – imagine that liquid wax has to flow through the form and reach the farthest part before it cools and hardens. Try to avoid making a piece where the wax would be expected to flow back on itself.

Making a silicone mould

1 Make a cone of modelling clay (this will be the sprue) and stick it to a square of Perspex or MDF. Attach the object to be cast to the cone. Make walls for the mould. These can be made from two pieces of aluminium that have been folded in half to form adjustable walls. Perspex can also be used. Alternatively, if you can find a suitably sized plastic box, this can be used for making the mould. The walls should extend at least 2.5cm (1in) above the object.

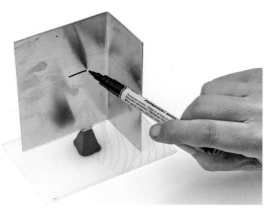

2 It is a good idea to mark the midpoint of the object on the inside of the walls of the mould while you can still see them.

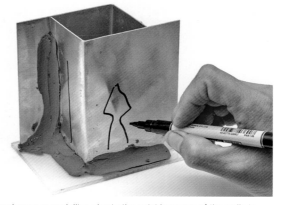

3 Apply wax or modelling clay to the outside seams of the walls to make sure that they are well sealed. It may also be useful to mark the way the object is facing on the outer walls.

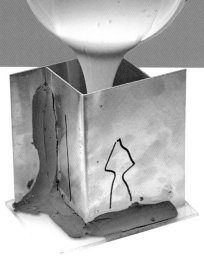

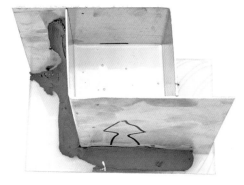

4 Because the silicone may have settled while in storage, stir it thoroughly with a metal or plastic stirrer while still in the pot. Mix the silicone and the catalyst according to the manufacturer's instructions. Make a note of how much silicone you use and how much catalyst you add. Stir it carefully, trying not to introduce too many bubbles to the mix. If you have access to a vacuum chamber, use it to remove any bubbles prior to pouring. Pour the mixture on to the object. It is best to pour it from a height in a thin stream.

5 Tilt the mould slightly so that the silicone can pour down the side of the wall in order to eliminate any bubbles that may get trapped. Tap the mould against the counter a few times to encourage any trapped air bubbles to emerge. Allow it to cure for 24 hours, after which time the rubber should be bouncy but solid.

6 Separate the mould from the walls and transfer any marks you made on the walls to the dry silicone. Using a very sharp new scalpel, cut through the rubber. The first few cuts you make down the sides of the mould should be zigzagged – this will help you to fit the mould back together perfectly once it has been opened.

7 Keep cutting until you make contact with the object inside. Pull the rubber to one side as you use the scalpel to free the object – remember that you will have to be able to get the wax version out of the mould without breaking it. Try to place the parting cut on the edge of the object to minimise casting lines.

8 Remove the object and the modelling clay sprue. Dust the inside of the mould with baby powder, then hold the mould wide open and blow most of it out again. You can now fit the pieces of the mould back together and pour in the melted casting wax. It is a good idea to use a rigid material such as Perspex held together with a rubber band to support the walls of the mould when doing this.

9 Once the mould is full, lift it up and tap it on a table a couple of times to release any air bubbles that may be trapped. Wait for the wax to solidify before trying to open the mould.

WHAT'S THE PROBLEM?

SHAPING

DECORATION

WIREWORK

CASTING

STONE SETTING

Vulcanised moulds

Vulcanised moulds are the most commonly used in jewellery casting because they are very durable, but the vulcaniser is an expensive piece of equipment, so making vulcanised moulds is usually a service performed by casting companies.

The object being vulcanised must be strong enough to stand the heat and pressure it will be exposed to, and must be capable of having a sprue soldered on to it – basically, it has to be made of metal. Vulcanised moulds have to be used in conjunction with a wax injector. Wax injectors have a chamber that heats up the wax, a pressurising system and a nozzle through which the wax is squirted.

Look at the object and decide how it should be sprued. Simple objects will only need one sprue; more complicated objects may need two or three pieces added to the central sprue. Deciding where to place the sprue is often a trade-off between putting it somewhere discrete on the object, and putting it somewhere sensible as far as casting is concerned. If the object has any solder joints, it is worth using easy solder or paste when soldering on the sprue.

The width of the sprue is dewtermined by the size of the nozzle on the wax injector that will be used to squirt wax into the mould. Some wax injectors have a particular shaped nozzle, and this shape should be replicated by attaching a positive version of it to the end of the sprue.

Making a vulcanised mould

1 Have a good look at the object and decide where the parting line should go – this is where the mould will be cut open. Sometimes a little wax escapes out of this cut, resulting in a raised line that has to be filed off after casting. Use a permanent pen to mark where you would like the line to go.

Parting line

Sprue

2 An aluminium mould holder is used to hold the object and contain the rubber. The mould holder will have a hole in it through which the sprue can be placed to hold the object in the middle of the mould. Moulding rubber comes in sheets that have to be cut to size and built up around the object in layers. Start by laying the object on to the rubber sheets and mark around it with a permanent pen.

3 Cut out the marked shape to create a space for inserting the piece being moulded.

4 Place the rubber sheet into the mould holder and place the object into the cutout space. Fill any negative spaces around the object with scraps of rubber until it is completely contained within the sheets of moulding rubber.

5 The final layer of rubber should stick up slightly above the top of the mould (by the thickness of one layer of rubber). This ensures that, when the rubber melts and is compressed, there will be no holes left around the object. The woven fabric covering the rubber can be left on the top and bottom layers (facing outwards); this provides a non-stick surface for the rubber.

6 Shake a little baby powder on to the rubber and sandwich the mould between two sheets of aluminium. When the vulcaniser it is at the correct temperature (154°C/310°F for Castaldo pink moulding rubber), place the mould holder into the vulcaniser and tighten the press until it is hand-tight.

7 Return to it after 5 minutes, loosen it a bit, then tighten it further. The mould should be ready in about 40 minutes, depending on how thick it is (7½ minutes per layer – it is important to make a note of how many layers have been used). Expect to see some rubber flowing out of the mould holder. Remove it carefully because it will be very hot. Run the mould under a cold tap until it can be handled and removed from the mould holder.

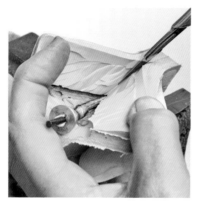

8 Cutting a vulcanised mould is quite a hard job. Use a very sharp scalpel, and hold the mould in a vice to free up both hands. Start cutting down the sides with zigzag strokes, then more carefully as the object is located. Look for the permanent pen line you made earlier and try to follow it with the scalpel.

9 Objects created from a mould in this way sometimes shrink slightly, but this is the best method for reproducing the master with perfect detail. Any errors in the master will be faithfully reproduced in the rubber.

Using a wax injector

1 Lightly dust the inside of the mould with baby powder, making sure it gets all over – this stops the wax from sticking. Support the mould on the top and bottom with two pieces of aluminium or Perspex. Grip these with both hands and apply light pressure when holding the mould.

2 Insert the nozzle of the injector into the mould and allow the hot wax to squirt in. Some injectors stop automatically; some you have to use experience to know when enough wax has gone in.

3 Hold the mould still for a few seconds to allow the wax to harden, then open the mould and extract the wax. Often the wax will come out more easily from one side of the mould than the other. Mark this side and use it from now on. Re-powder the mould before injecting again.

WHAT'S THE PROBLEM?

SHAPING

DECORATION

WIREWORK

CASTING

STONE SETTING

Casting techniques

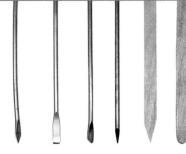

THE PROBLEM

Some parts on the carved wax model are very hard to reach in order to smooth down

Caused by: It is hard to get tools into every part of the object. Lost wax casting is very accurate, so any imperfections in the wax model will be reflected in the cast object.

THE SOLUTION

Improvise your tools: It is worth persevering with these parts at the wax stage because dealing with such areas after casting is very difficult. This may mean improvising with whatever you can find, and possibly making tools to get into small areas. Try broken saw blades, pins, coffee stirrers (they can be sharpened), small riffler files and dental picks. Also try using small rubber burrs on a mircromotor or pendant drill.

▲ Make some improvised tools, such as sharpened coffee stirrers and flattened and sharpened wires.

THE PROBLEM

The wax being worked on has snapped or a mistake has been made

Caused by: Wax is quite brittle, green carving wax particularly so; the wrong part has been carved or burred off accidentally.

▲ Broken wax model

▲ Use a soldering probe to melt the wax on each side of the break.

THE SOLUTIONS

Join snapped pieces together again: The wax can be patched together again with the help of a torch and soldering probe. Have some scrap wax on hand, preferably a long thin bit. Butt the two broken pieces against each other and apply the hot probe to melt them together (go right around the seam). Then hold the scrap piece of wax close to the join and use the hot probe to melt some wax on to the join. Allow to cool for 24 hours before continuing, then file back until smooth and finish with wire wool.

Repair the mistake: It is possible to melt wax and fill any errors. Before dripping wax into a mistake, slightly melt the wax on/beneath the area so that the new melted wax will stick to it, otherwise any wax you drip on can easily come off again. Allow to cool properly, then file down and recarve.

▲ Join the snapped pieces and melt scrap wax all around the outside of the join.

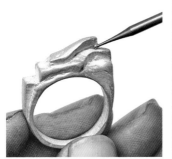

THE PROBLEM

When using hot tools to model wax, the wax keeps going stringy

Caused by: The tool is not hot enough, so the wax is solidifying as it is worked.

THE SOLUTION

Heat the tool up more: If the wax starts smoking, though, it is a bit too hot.

◄ Wax can go stringy when not heated enough.

THE PROBLEM

The investment plaster will not come off the cast piece

Caused by: Sometimes investment plaster can be very stubborn, particularly on pieces cast in brass or gilding metal.

THE SOLUTION

Try different tools to clean it up:
■ Put it in a strong concentration of hot pickle for an hour or so, then clean with a wire brush on a pendant drill or micromotor.
■ Use a tiny burr to dig it out.
■ If you have access to one, an ultrasonic machine may vibrate out the plaster.

▲ Use a tiny burr to clean off the plaster from small crevices.

THE PROBLEM

The casting has porosity holes

Caused by: The wax may not have properly burned out of the investment mould; the molten metal may have been overheated when cast; or too high a percentage of recycled silver has been used, which has introduced impurities to the alloy.

THE SOLUTIONS

Fill with solder: Very slight porosity can be cured by flooding the pit with hard solder and emerying it back, then polish in the usual way.
Return to the casting company: Lots of pits on the surface may well be an indicator that there will be holes throughout the casting, making it weak, so the piece should be returned to the casting company. Unfortunately, sometimes porosity only shows up at the polishing stage. Before selecting a casting company, ask fellow jewellers who they recommend.

▲ Flood the hole with hard solder.

▲ Use emery paper to sand back the solder.

WHAT'S THE PROBLEM?

SHAPING

DECORATION

WIREWORK

CASTING

STONE SETTING

THE PROBLEM

There are long fins down either side of cuttlefish cast

Caused by: This is known as flashing. Both halves of the mould are not meeting properly because they were not sanded flat prior to pouring the metal.

▲ Fins of metal along the sides of the cast are known as flashing.

THE SOLUTION

Re-sand the mould: It may be necessary to make another mould, but re-sanding both sides accurately is worth a try. Attach some emery paper to a piece of glass or Perspex using double-sided tape or spray mount. Use this to sand the halves. Don't go too far or the casting void will become very flat and may not register properly.

▲ Sand both sides of the cuttlefish mould flat.

THE PROBLEM

The cuttlefish cast object is uneven

Caused by: The mould has come out of registration.

THE SOLUTION

Adjust the registration: Reinsert the master object, fit the two halves of the mould back together and check that the registration marks still line up. Open the mould and insert registration rods. Before pouring the next casting, make sure that the registration marks you made line up properly.

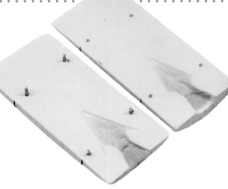

▲ Insert rods to help register the two halves of the mould.

THE PROBLEM

The object is too thick for the available cuttlefish

Caused by: The master is too high to allow enough moulding material on the top and bottom of the mould.

THE SOLUTION

Join two cuttlefish together: Use two cuttlefish bones instead of cutting one in half. Flatten the top section of both of them and fit together.

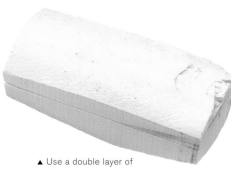

▲ Use a double layer of cuttlefish to cast deep objects.

WHAT'S THE PROBLEM?

SHAPING

DECORATION

WIREWORK

CASTING

STONE SETTING

Mould making

THE PROBLEM

There are bubbles in the silicone mould

Caused by: Lots of tiny bubbles are the result of air being introduced when the silicone was mixed. Random bubbles may have been trapped when the mixture was poured.

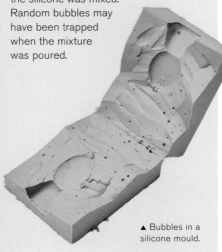

▲ Bubbles in a silicone mould.

THE SOLUTION

Mix carefully: Care should be taken at all times not to introduce air to the mix. The catalyst should be stirred in gently in a circular motion. If available, use a vacuum chamber to remove all the bubbles.

Try it and see: It is always worth testing a mould by pouring the wax in anyway. The result might not be as bad as you feared. Sometimes the top of the mould is bubbly because the bubbles rose to the surface but did not burst.

▲ Bubbles on a cast piece.

File off or remake: If you go ahead and try making a casting, you may be able to file or burr off the bubbles. If it is too bad, the mould must be remade.

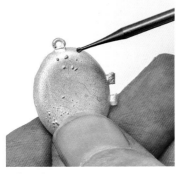

▲ Use a burr to remove bubbles from casting.

THE PROBLEM

Silicone has not hardened

Caused by: It is most likely that the catalyst to rubber ratio has been miscalculated. Check the use-by date on the container.

THE SOLUTIONS

Wait longer: Wait another 24 hours to see if it sets – temperature and humidity can affect setting time.

▼ Always double-check your catalyst to rubber ratio carefully.

Check the ratio: Refer to your notes and check that the ratio of catalyst to rubber is correct. A commonly made mistake is if the instructions say the catalyst ratio should be 1 in 5. This does not mean 5 per cent; it equates to 20 per cent. There is a certain amount of latitude allowed with catalysts, but if you have seriously underestimated it, the mould will never set, so you should clean it off and start again. Adding too much catalyst to the mix can cause the mould to become brittle and tear easily over time.

THE PROBLEM

Haven't mixed up the right amount of silicone

Caused by: It can be hard to estimate the volume required. Although you don't want to waste materials, it is always advisable to make too much rather than not enough.

▶ Leave excess silicone to set and then remove it in one piece.

THE SOLUTIONS

Make more: The object should be covered by about 2.5cm (1in) of silicone. If you have made too little, quickly make some more and pour it on.
Leave it to set: If you have made too much silicone, leave it in the jug or bowl. It can be pulled out in one piece once it has set.

THE PROBLEM

Vulcanised mould has horizontal lines on it or gaps in the cavities

Caused by: The rubber has not been packed tightly enough, so gaps have been left. The protective plastic between layers may have been left on, or the surface of the layers of rubber may have become contaminated with oil or powder. The vulcaniser may not have reached the correct temperature, or the mould was not left in it long enough.

▶ Horizontal lines can indicate that the rubber sheets are not packed tightly enough.

▶ Well-packed mould

THE SOLUTION

Start again: If this has happened, the only option is to start again.
■ Make sure the mould is adequately packed, pushing small scraps of rubber into all areas of the mould. Use a metal probe to push these right up against the object.

■ Make sure that the rubber is clean.
■ Check that both top and bottom plates on the vulcaniser are working and that they are achieving the correct temperature.

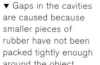

▼ Gaps in the cavities are caused because smaller pieces of rubber have not been packed tightly enough around the object.

WHAT'S THE PROBLEM?

SHAPING

DECORATION

WIREWORK

CASTING

STONE SETTING

THE PROBLEM

Rubber mould is curling up

Caused by: This sometimes happens with pink moulding rubber.

▶ Two-colour rubber mould, with cheaper rubber on the outside.

THE SOLUTIONS

Flatten with a weight: Place a weight, such as a book, on it overnight.

Combine white and pink rubber: When making a mould, use the cheaper white rubber on the outer layers and the more expensive no-shrink pink for the inner section that is in contact with the object being cast.

THE PROBLEM

When soldering on the sprue, the other solder joints are melting

Caused by: Sometimes soldering the sprue on is one joint too far.

THE SOLUTION

Use the right solder: This is a common problem. If a piece is being constructed as a casting master, try to use hard solder on it as much as possible. Protect any delicate solder joints with heat-resistant paste or gel. The sprue can then be attached with easy solder or paste.

▲ Protect previous solder joints with heat-resistant gel.

THE PROBLEM

The sprue has become detached under the pressure of the vulcaniser

Caused by: The sprue was not properly soldered on.

THE SOLUTION

Make a test run: This will result in the rubber filling the space that the sprue would have made. It is worth trying to cut out a channel in the rubber where the sprue would have been and testing the mould with the wax injector to see if it will work. If not, you will have to start again.

▲ Cut the rubber out of the sprue channel.

THE PROBLEM

Vulcanised mould is very hard to cut open

Caused by: The model may have been overpacked. In an effort to ensure that the model has enough rubber, it is possible to overpack it by putting an extra layer on and overtightening the press. This can result in a very dense, springy mould that is hard to cut.

THE SOLUTIONS

Cutting tips:
- Slightly warm the mould before trying to cut it. Use a brand new scalpel.
- Dip the scalpel regularly into a solution of liquid detergent and water to lubricate the blade.

▲ Dip the scalpel in warm soapy water when cutting the mould.

- Hold the mould in a vice to free up both your hands, so that one hand can be parting the mould while the other cuts. Be very careful when doing this.

▲ Hold the mould in a vice to leave both hands free for the job.

THE PROBLEM

Injected wax casting is not complete or snaps when being removed from mould

THE CAUSES

Incomplete wax: Either not enough wax has been injected, or the wax solidified before it reached the end, forming a block that prevented more wax from going through.

Snapped wax: Wax has cooled too much and become brittle. The mould may have been badly cut, trapping a piece of wax and making it hard to extract.

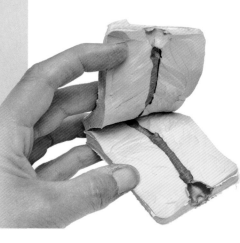

▶ Injected wax has not reached the end of the mould.

THE SOLUTIONS

Incomplete wax:
- Try again, this time making sure that enough wax is injected.
- This problem often happens with the first injection when the mould is cold. Warm the mould slightly if it happens again.

Snapped wax:
- Waxes can be most easily removed when they are very slightly bendy, but make sure you straighten them out while they are still malleable. Practice will tell you how long to leave the mould before pulling the wax out.
- If the mould has been badly cut, trapping a piece where it is hard to extract, try making a scalpel cut in the mould to allow this area to open more fully. With the next injection, try opening the mould from the other side. If this works, mark the best side with a permanent pen.

▲ Use a scalpel to cut into awkward areas to help them open more fully.

WHAT'S THE PROBLEM?

SHAPING

DECORATION

WIREWORK

CASTING

STONE SETTING

THE PROBLEM

Fault showing on every wax

Caused by: Any mistake on the master will be faithfully reproduced every time. Sometimes the moulding rubber has been contaminated – a thread from the fabric that covers one side of it or a scrap of the protective plastic from the other side will spoil every wax.

THE SOLUTION

Clean up or remake: Check the master and the mould to see where the fault lies. Decide if it can be easily cleaned up once cast. If not, make it again.

▶ Try using a buff stick to clean up flaws on the cast piece.

THE PROBLEM

There are large fins down the side of the waxes

Caused by: This is known as flashing, caused by wax squirting out of the parting line on the mould.

THE SOLUTION

Adjust the injection process:
■ Reduce the air pressure on the injector.

■ Hold the mould more firmly together when injecting, and keep the pressure up for a couple of minutes while the wax cools.

◀ Fins of wax at the parting line of the mould are known as flashing.

THE PROBLEM

Air bubbles in the wax

Caused by: The temperature of the wax may be too high or too low. The wax level may be too low and the air pressure too high. Air might have been introduced via the nozzle.

THE SOLUTIONS

Fine-tune the injector: Check the wax temperature, pressure and level, and adjust as necessary.

Position the nozzle properly: Make sure that the mould is firmly placed against the nozzle so that no air can get in.

▲ Air bubbles in the injected wax model.

CHAPTER 6

STONE SETTING

The very word jewellery tends to conjure up images of treasure and fabulous jewels – multicoloured gems set in a Cartier necklace, the sparkle of a debutante's tiara, Elizabeth Taylor's diamonds, the Queen's crown. Many jewellers find stone setting quite daunting, and many outsource this aspect of their work – and it is true that professional stone setters spend years as apprentices to gain their skills. But with care and concentration, good results are perfectly achievable. A few of the easiest techniques to learn are documented in this chapter – these just scratch the surface of another huge jewellery-related adventure.

Bezel setting

A bezel is a band of metal that sits around a stone. The metal is then pushed over, or rubbed over, the edge of the stone to hold the stone securely in position. This setting method is commonly used to secure cabochon stones but can also be used for faceted gemstones.

▲ ELIZAVETA GNATCHENKO
An opulent mixture of stones and setting and stringing techniques are employed in this bracelet.

Bezel setting a cabochon is the stone-setting project most frequently taught to beginners, and is the perfect introduction to the art of mount making and stone setting. Cabochons are stones that have been smoothly polished (that is, they do not have facets like diamonds). They have a flat base and a domed top, the height of which can vary.

Setting a round cabochon

Select a stone with a flat base with no bevel. Make sure that it sits level on a flat surface. Look at the stone and estimate how high the bezel should be. It should be high enough to hold the stone, but not so high that it obscures it too much.

Making the bezel Cut a strip of metal of between 0.5mm and 0.8mm thick to form the bezel. If you are mathematically minded, you can multiply the diameter of the stone by pi (3.14) and allow a little extra for the width of the saw blade. Alternatively, cut more than you need and wrap it into a spiral into which the stone fits, then saw through the overlapping ends.

Ready-made bezel strip is commercially available in various metals. It is generally quite thin, and as such, rather easy to melt (but very easy to push over). Decorative gallery wire can also be used.

Solder the bezel together and make it perfectly round on a small mandrel. Check that the stone fits perfectly inside the bezel. If there is a gap through which you can see daylight, saw it open at the solder joint and re-solder – often just the width of the saw blade is enough to tighten the bezel. If it is too tight, hammer it on the mandrel to stretch it, moving it around to make sure that the metal thickness remains consistent. Check the fit frequently. The stone should fit into the bezel from above with no resistance.

▲ Cut a metal strip that will fit around the stone with an overlap.

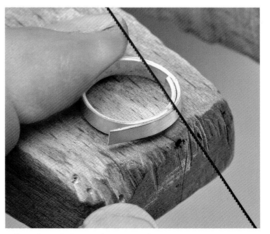

▲ Saw through the overlapping ends.

▲ Check that the stones fits into the bezel perfectly.

► Cut a square of sheet metal slightly larger than the bezel.

▼ Solder together and then saw off the excess.

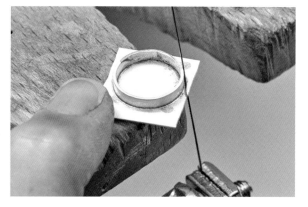

Completing the mount Cut a small flat square of sheet metal between about 0.5mm and 0.8mm thick. It should be slightly larger than the bezel. Apply flux to the underside of the bezel and position it on the base sheet. Arrange four pallions of solder at the cardinal points on the outside of the bezel. Heat until the solder runs right around the base of the bezel.

The area around the bezel can then be pierced away. This is why the solder is placed around the outside – if any pallions failed to melt on the inside of the bezel, it would prevent the stone from sitting properly. Take care when piercing it that the saw is kept perpendicular to the base piece. Saw as close to the edge as possible, then file and emery off any excess metal.

At this point a jump ring or bail could be added, the setting could be mounted on a ring or ear posts soldered on. If you cannot to resist the temptation to fit the stone into the piece at this stage, place a piece of dental floss underneath it with the edges sticking over the side. This provides a handy way to extract the stone if it is a tight fit.

Decide now whether you want to create an opening in the back of the setting to let some light in. If so, set dividers to the required width and scribe a line using the inside of the setting as a guide. Drill a hole near this line, insert the saw blade and pierce out the hole. File and sand.

Setting the stone To set the stone, hold the piece in a ring clamp if possible, or fix it in some setter's wax on a dopping stick. If it is a large pendant, it might be possible to hold it with your hands and brace it against the edge of the bench peg. Thermolock is a substance that becomes plastic when heated in a microwave or in boiling water, but sets solid when cold. It is very useful for stone setting because it does not stick to the work as readily as setting cement.

Fit the stone into the bezel and make sure that it is pushed right into the setting and is sitting flat. Start pushing the bezel towards the stone with a setting tool. The setting tool should be made of tool steel or silver steel, and its end should be gently curved. It should be set into a graver handle so that it can be comfortably pushed with the hand.

Every push of the bezel should be matched with a push on the opposite side – north then south, east then west and so on. Start pushing with the tool at about 90 degrees to the bezel, then angle it upwards to about 45 degrees to push the metal on to the stone. Push firmly, but not with extreme force. Try not to let the tool slip. Keep going around the stone until any crinkles and irregularities have been pushed out.

Run a needle file carefully around the edge at about a 45-degree angle, taking care not to scratch the stone. Finally, run a burnishing tool around the setting in an action similar to that of peeling an apple. To make sure that the setting functions properly and to ensure the longevity of your piece, test the setting by pressing some beeswax on to the centre of the stone and pulling it up sharply.

► Use a setting tool to push the bezel over the stone.

▼ Run a burnisher around the bezel to finish.

WHAT'S THE PROBLEM?

SHAPING

DECORATION

WIREWORK

CASTING

STONE SETTING

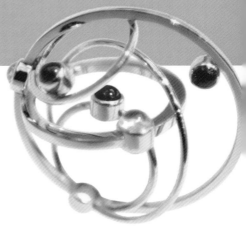

Setting a square cabochon

1 Cut two strips of bezel. Using an engineer's square, scribe a point slightly longer than the length of the stone on each strip. The rest of each strip should be considerably longer than the stone. Use the edge of a square needle file to cut a V-shaped groove at the marked point in each strip.

2 Fold each strip at the groove to a 90-degree angle and solder it for strength. Fit each strip against the stone and file off any excess metal, so that one of the legs on each strip is exactly the same length as the stone.

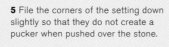

3 Place the two right-angled strips against the stone, with the long legs pointing in opposite directions. Adjust them until the strips fit tightly, and mark where the outside edge of the short legs meet the long ones.

4 Remove the stone and arrange the strips on a soldering mat. Pieces of binding wire can be stuck into the soldering mat to hold the setting in place. Flux and solder, then cut off the excess metal on the long legs. Solder on to the base plate as you would for a round stone.

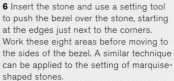

5 File the corners of the setting down slightly so that they do not create a pucker when pushed over the stone.

6 Insert the stone and use a setting tool to push the bezel over the stone, starting at the edges just next to the corners. Work these eight areas before moving to the sides of the bezel. A similar technique can be applied to the setting of marquise-shaped stones.

▲ ELIZAVETA GNATCHENKO
Tube settings have been used to great effect in this intricate ring.

Tube or chenier setting

Tube can also be used to form the bezel for a cabochon or faceted stone. Tube is most easily cut with the aid of a chenier block, which is the best way to keep the ends straight and perpendicular to the walls.

The stone needs to have an inner ledge, or bearing, for the girdle of the stone (if faceted) or base of the stone (cabochon) to rest on. This can be achieved by soldering a narrower tube inside the setting, or by using a setting burr to burr off some of the tube wall. You have to decide in advance which method will be employed in order to buy tube of the correct dimensions. If another piece of tube is to be soldered inside the setting tube, the larger of the two should be of exactly the same diameter as the stone to be set. Like a telescope, the bearing tube should fit exactly inside the setting tube.

If you are going to burr out a bearing, then tube with a slightly smaller inside diameter than the stone. Sufficient wall thickness will be needed to allow some metal to be removed. If you are setting a 3mm stone, use a tube with an external diameter of 3.5mm and an internal diameter of 2.6mm. This will allow plenty of metal to drill into for the seat and 0.25mm to rub over the stone.

Making a tube setting

1 Solder the setting to the piece of jewellery or attach a jump ring. Select a round burr exactly the same size as the stone or slightly smaller. Set the burr in a pin vice and lubricate it. Keeping it absolutely straight, burr out a space for the stone.

2 Once you have opened up the space with the round burr, switch to a setting burr. Setting burrs tend to clog up more easily than round ones, so it is a good idea to start with a round burr. Check the fit of the stone regularly. The girdle of the stone should be just below the edge of the tube.

3 Make sure that the stone will sit straight in the setting. An easy way to pick up the stone is by forming a little cone of beeswax between the fingers until it melts slightly and gets sticky. Stones can also be picked up by licking the end of the setting tool if they are fairly small.

4 When the stone is in the right position, it can be set. Butt one side of the setting against the bench peg or the edge of the bench and push the opposite side with a setting tool. Rotate the setting 180 degrees and repeat. Rotate 90 degrees and continue around until the stone is firmly set.

5 Run around the edge of the bezel with a burnisher.

6 Alternatively, bezel-setting tools are available that are very useful for pushing the metal over fairly small stones. They work particularly well with tube settings. They are like doming punches in reverse, with a concave space at the end of the punch. Place the end of the tool over the setting and rotate simultaneously to push the metal over the stone and burnish it.

▲ Tube-set rings with different height settings.

WHAT'S THE PROBLEM?

SHAPING

DECORATION

WIREWORK

CASTING

STONE SETTING

Flush and prong setting

Flush setting uses the metal of the piece itself as a method to hold the stone. Prong setting creates a pronged mount and is the best way to show off the light-reflecting qualities of a facted stone.

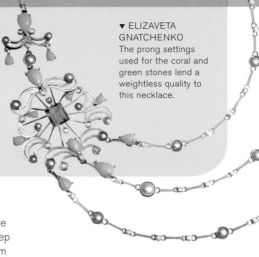

▼ ELIZAVETA GNATCHENKO
The prong settings used for the coral and green stones lend a weightless quality to this necklace.

Flush setting a stone

The stone is set level with the metal, just punctuating the surface. The metal must be thicker than the stone is deep or else the cullet of the stone will poke out of the bottom and lacerate the wearer's finger.

▲ SHAROL HSU
The flush-set pink tourmaline stone augments the larger tension-set piece of smoky quartz.

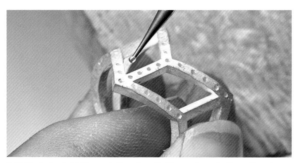

1 Drill a hole right through the piece in the centre of where the stone will sit. The width of this hole should be around three-quarters of the diameter of the stone. Use a round burr the same size as the stone to open up this hole to accept the stone.

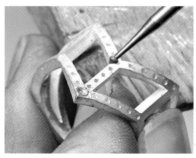

2 Neaten up the seat with a seating burr, making sure that it is goes into the hole straight.

3 Pick up the stone on a cone of beeswax and fit the stone into the setting; the girdle should be below the surface of the metal.

4 Using the side of a small polished burnisher, press the cardinal points close to the stone to push the metal over the girdle.

5 Raise the burnisher slightly and move it all around the edge of the stone a couple of times. Raise the burnisher until it is perpendicular and keep going around the edge of the stone using the blunt point of the tool. Finish by going around the edge carefully with a small piece of emery paper to remove any scratches.

Making a prong setting

Also known as a claw or basket setting, this type of setting holds the stone in a little basket made from wire. It is delicate and open and very fiddly to make, but don't let that put you off – just reserve its use for larger stones.

1 Make a jump ring with an outside diameter exactly the same as that of the stone. The girdle of the stone will rest on this. It is important to keep the wire straight at all times and to be as accurate as possible. Make another jump ring slightly smaller than the first one. Solder them closed.

2 Cut two lengths of wire about 35mm (1½in) long. Find the midpoint of each and bend them up using round-nose pliers. Bend them near the end of the pliers so that the angle is quite acute.

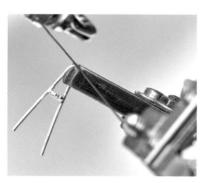

3 Using a round needle file or gapping file, make a notch on the outside edge of the jump rings on the place they were soldered shut. Turn each 180 degrees and repeat. Turn 90 degrees and repeat until you have four little grooves on each jump ring for the prongs to sit in. Slip the smaller jump ring inside one of the V-shaped prongs. Make sure it sits straight and then solder it together with hard solder. Cut a 1mm gap in the apex of the V shape to make space for the second wire to fit in.

4 Slide the second wire into position so that it sits in the notches on the jump ring. Solder the bottom point together where the wires meet and then solder the prongs on to the jump ring.

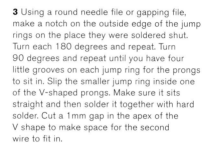

5 Straighten up the prongs and slide the larger jump ring into the basket. Make sure it is sitting straight and parallel with the lower one, and that the wires are all sitting in the grooves. Solder in place, then pickle. Use a round burr the same size as the stone on the top jump ring to give the stone an angled seat to rest on. Follow this up with a setting burr.

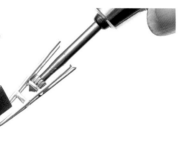

6 Put the stone in the setting and cut off the top wires so that they are at the same height as the pavilion of the stone. File and sand them flat.

7 Saw off the wires at the bottom, level with the bottom jump ring, and file them smooth. File off some of the wire on the outside of the prongs so that they will be easier to bend over. At this point, the setting can either be attached to a ring or made into a pendant or earring.

8 Place the stone in the setting, making sure it is straight, and mark where the girdle hits the wires. Use a fraise burr to cut a small groove on the inside of each prong to allow the prong to bend neatly around the stone.

9 Put the stone in the setting. If everything is working perfectly, it should click into the prongs. Use pliers to push the opposing prongs together, then move on to a push tool to set them firmly over the stone. Smooth the tips of the prongs with a burnisher.

THE PROBLEM

The stone is too large for the bezel and will not fit in

Caused by: The bezel was too small before it was soldered on. It may have stretched on to the stone when placed over it, but it is better to put the stone into the bezel, as would be the case after soldering.

THE SOLUTION

Minor adjustments: Meticulous checking should have taken place prior to soldering the piece, so any discrepancy should be minimal. Sometimes all that is required is running a burnisher around the inside edge. A riffler file run around the bottom may free up enough space for the stone to sit nicely. Make sure the stone is sitting right at the bottom and not at an angle before setting. If this does not work, you will have to remake the setting with a larger bezel.

▲ Run a burnisher around the inside edge.

THE PROBLEM

The stone keeps moving in the setting

Caused by: The bezel is too big for the stone. If the bezel is pushed over a large gap, the whole setting can look off-balance.

THE SOLUTION

Make a judgement: A value judgement has to be made about whether the space is too large to get away with (ideally, the stone should fit perfectly). You may have to start again.

◄ The stone is smaller than the bezel.

◄ Perfect size bezel for the stone.

THE PROBLEM

The stone has pinged out when being set

Caused by: The stone has not been pushed in sufficiently, possibly because the bezel is too tight; the bezel may be too short for the stone.

THE SOLUTIONS

Make a higher bezel: Measure the height of the bezel and look at this in relation to the stone. If it is too short, you will have to remake the setting with a higher bezel.

Open up a tight bezel: If the setting is too tight, try opening it up with a burnisher. When inserting the stone, push it down firmly with the wooden handle of the pusher and make sure that it is sitting straight in the setting.

► Use the handle of the pusher tool to push the stone down firmly in a tight bezel.

THE PROBLEM

The stone is jammed in the setting

Caused by: Forgetting to place a length of dental floss under the stone for easy removal.

THE SOLUTIONS

Pull out with beeswax: This is something of a rite of passage. Try using a little cone of beeswax that has been warmed between the fingers. Apply it to the stone and jerk it upwards sharply.

Drill a hole and push it out: If that fails, carefully drill a hole in the underside of the bezel (if it is for a ring, this hole can be covered by the ring shank later). Push the stone out with a scribe or drill bit.

◀ Use a cone of warmed beeswax to try to lift out the stone.

▶ Drill a hole in the setting and push out the stone.

THE PROBLEM

The setting has come off the ring when being set

Caused by: It was not properly soldered on and could not withstand the pressure applied during setting.

THE SOLUTIONS

Remove stone and re-solder: Try to extract the stone from the setting by running a scribe around the bezel, undoing the work of the setting tool. If this works, the setting may still be useable and can be re-soldered on to the shank.

Cut out stone and start again: If the stone cannot be removed, saw the bezel apart and remake.

▲ Run a scribe around the bezel to help remove the stone.

THE PROBLEM

A gap has opened up at the bottom of the bezel when the stone was being set

Caused by: Solder did not flow all the way around the joint.

THE SOLUTION

Saw out the stone and remake: You will have to saw the stone out of this setting and make a new one.

▲ Saw open the setting and remove the stone.

Gap at bottom of bezel

WHAT'S THE PROBLEM?

SHAPING

DECORATION

WIREWORK

CASTING

STONE SETTING

THE PROBLEM

Can't get the bezel walls to meet the stone

Caused by: The bezel is too thick or is not being pushed hard enough.

THE SOLUTIONS

Thin out the top edge: Heavy bezels can look really good, but can be very hard to push over. Run a flat needle file around the very top of the outside of the setting at a 45-degree angle. This thins the metal, making it easier to push over, and adds a chamfered edge to the setting.

Anneal prior to setting: For very heavy bezels, it is worth getting the piece up to the polishing stage and then carefully annealing the bezel to get maximum plasticity before setting.

Hammer with a chasing tool: If it is still proving difficult, place the setting in a vice and hammer the bezel towards the stone gently using a chasing tool. Use the same technique as you would when setting with a hand tool (that is, use the cardinal points). Work slowly and carefully and hammer gently to avoid damaging the stone.

▲ Thin out the top edge by filing at a 45-degree angle.

▲ Holding the setting in a vice, hammer the bezel towards the stone.

▲ Finish by running a burnisher around the setting.

THE PROBLEM

The stone rocks and moves when being set

Caused by: The bottom of the stone is slightly convex.

THE SOLUTION

Add a jump ring to the base of the bezel: Bend up some round wire so that it fits snugly at the bottom of the bezel, test that the stone is sitting still and then remove the stone and solder the wire in place. Set as normal.

▶ Insert a jump ring to tighten up the setting.

WHAT'S THE PROBLEM?

SHAPING

DECORATION

WIREWORK

CASTING

STONE SETTING

THE PROBLEM

Push tool keeps slipping off the bezel

Caused by: A polished tool will tend to slip under pressure.

▶ Marks left by adding a key to the push tool will need to be sanded off.

THE SOLUTION

Add a key to the push tool: Professional stone setters use highly polished push tools. These will leave no marks on the metal but are very prone to slipping. As a beginner, put a slight key on the tool by putting it in a vice and hitting it lightly with a rough file. This may deposit slight marks on the bezel, but these can be sanded off.

▶ Use a rough file to apply a slight key to the end of the push tool.

THE PROBLEM

As the stone is being set, the corners of the square bezel are getting longer

Caused by: The bezel is slightly too large. As it is pushed on to the stone along the sides, it is stretching out towards the corners.

▶ The corners flare out from the stone.

THE SOLUTIONS

File back: Try filing back the corners and see how they look. The setting may be salvageable.

Use thicker metal: Making the bezel of slightly thicker metal can help to prevent this, and should it happen, allows a certain thickness that can be filed back.

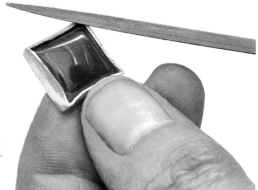

▶ File back the corners of the bezel.

THE PROBLEM

The stone is sitting too far down in the tube setting or is not sitting straight

Caused by: The setting burr has gone too deeply into the tube. The seat is not parallel with the top of the setting.

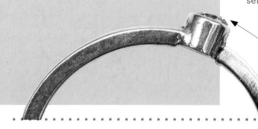

Stone sitting too deeply in the setting.

THE SOLUTION

Remove the stone, file and re-burr:

■ It might be necessary to file the top of the setting where the metal has been rubbed over and then push the stone from the other side of the setting to get it out.

■ If the setting is too deep for the stone, file some metal off the top and then carefully re-burr. Make sure the burr is held absolutely straight in relation to the setting.

■ If the setting is askew, see how the stone fits after filing the top edge straight. If necessary, burr out some more metal – but not too much!

▲ File the top edge of the setting straight.

▲ Use a setting burr to remove enough metal for the stone.

▲ Take care to keep the burr absolutely straight.

The stone is slightly askew in the tube setting rather than straight.

THE PROBLEM

The tube wall is too thick to set a small stone

Caused by: If setting very small stones, it can be difficult to find fine enough tube relative to the stone size.

THE SOLUTION

File at an angle: File the top of the tube to a 45-degree angle and anneal before setting. This should make it easier to push over. Using a bezel-setting tool may also make setting easier.

▲ File the top of the tube at a 45-degree angle to make it thinner and easier to push over.

fix-its

Flush and prong setting

THE PROBLEM

The stone falls out

Caused by: The seat was not set deeply enough, or the burr used was slightly too large.

THE SOLUTIONS

Burr a deeper setting: Put the stone back in the setting and see if the girdle is 0.2mm below the surface. If not, burr a bit deeper.
Reset or find a new stone: If the burr was slightly too large, try annealing the metal and resetting the stone, using more pressure at the first stage to secure the stone. Failing that, find a wider stone.

▲ Burr out a deeper setting.

THE PROBLEM

The stone is sitting too deep in the setting

Caused by: The setting burr went down too far.

This stone is sitting too deep within the tube setting.

THE SOLUTIONS

File it back: Leave the stone in place and file the area around it if possible. It might be necessary to remove the stone, file the area back and reset it.
Solder wire into the setting: If the setting is a write-off, remove the stone, drill out a hole and solder a piece of wire into it. File and sand this back, then reset the stone.

▲ Solder a piece of wire into the setting to give a higher seating for the stone.

THE PROBLEM

There are scratches around the setting or on the stone

Caused by: The setting tool has slipped and may be too sharp. Some stones are too soft to be set in this way.

THE SOLUTIONS

Check the tool: Check the surface of the setting tool; it should be blunt and polished.
Burnish the setting: Rub the scratches with a polished burnisher rather than using a file, which might damage the setting.
Change the stone: Don't use any stones below 8 on the Mohs hardness scale as they may be damaged by the steel burnisher. Try to find a harder stone, or a plentiful supply of softer stones.

▲ Use a burnisher to remove scratches from the metal setting.

THE PROBLEM

The two jump rings are not parallel

Caused by: One may have slipped when being soldered, or perhaps the first one was not straight to start with.

THE SOLUTION

Remove the ring and re-solder: Decide which one is the offender. Hold the piece in a third hand and remove the offending jump ring. Pickle and rinse it, then re-solder it.

▲ Hold the setting in a third hand to remove the jump ring.

THE PROBLEM

When soldering the jump ring on to the setting, the tips of one of the prongs has melted

Caused by: While concentrating on the area being soldered, the hottest part of the torch was doing damage elsewhere.

THE SOLUTIONS

Cut off the damage if possible: Put the stone in the setting and see if the damaged area of the prong will be cut off anyway.

Start again: If the damaged prong is going to be apparent, it is best to start again because this type of setting is very labour intensive.

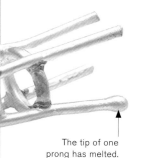

The tip of one prong has melted.

▲ You may be able to cut off the melted tip and still use the setting.

THE PROBLEM

Hard to saw out the centre of the V-shaped wire

Caused by: The wire moves too much and makes it impossible to cut.

THE SOLUTION

Grip it with parallel pliers: Grip the wire in some parallel pliers at the point where it needs to be sawn. Hold them firmly and saw through the wire using the pliers as a guide.

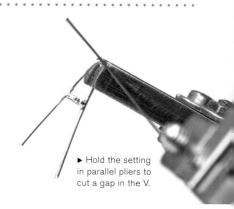

▶ Hold the setting in parallel pliers to cut a gap in the V.

WHAT'S THE PROBLEM?

SHAPING

DECORATION

WIREWORK

CASTING

STONE SETTING

THE PROBLEM

The larger jump ring will not sit straight on the prongs

Caused by: The prongs are too splayed out. The notches in the jump ring are not pronounced enough.

◄ Slanted jump ring

THE SOLUTIONS

Squeeze the prongs closer: Squeeze the prongs together a little so that they make good contact with the jump ring.
Increase the notch depth: Use a gapping or needle file to increase the depth of the notches on the jump ring.

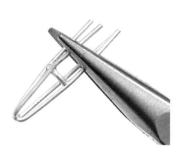

▲ Squeeze the prongs together.

▲ Use a file to deepen the notches on the ring.

THE PROBLEM

The prongs look bulgy and are not holding the stone firmly

Caused by: The little nick in the prongs where the girdle sits might be at the wrong height, or too shallow. The prongs might need to be reduced by filing them. The seating jump ring might be too large.

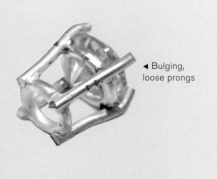

◄ Bulging, loose prongs

THE SOLUTIONS

Straighten and re-burr: Have a look at where the prongs curve over the girdle. If the little nick is at the wrong height or insufficient, straighten the prongs carefully and go in again with the fraise burr.

▲ Straighten the prongs.

◄ Then use a fraise burr to perfect the setting.

File the prongs down: If the prongs look too bulky, remove the stone, straighten the prongs and file them down on the outer edge, then reset.
Adjust jump ring size: The whole construction of this setting hinges around the seating jump ring being accurately sized to match the size of the stone. If the jump ring is slightly too small for the stone, there is some room for manoeuvre – the bulk of the prongs that will be removed on the outside could be removed from the inside of the setting. However, if this jump ring is too large, there is not much hope of the prongs holding the stone properly. This might have to be chalked up to experience. Making anything is always easier second time round.

Measurements and conversions

Ring sizes

UK	US	EUROPE	RING BLANK LENGTH		INSIDE DIAMETER	
			mm	inches	mm	inches
A	½	38	40.8	1.61	12.1	0.47
B	1	39	42.0	1.65	12.4	0.49
C	1½	40.5	43.2	1.70	12.8	0.50
D	2	42.5	44.5	1.75	13.2	0.52
E	2½	43	45.8	1.80	13.6	0.54
F	3	44	47.2	1.85	14.0	0.55
G	3¼	45	48.3	1.90	14.2	0.56
H	3¾	46.5	49.5	1.95	14.6	0.57
I	4¼	48	50.8	2.00	15.0	0.59
J	4¾	49	52.7	2.05	15.4	0.61
K	5¼	50	53.4	2.10	15.8	0.62
L	5¾	51.5	54.6	2.15	16.2	0.64
M	6¼	53	56.0	2.20	16.6	0.65
N	6¾	54	57.8	2.25	17.0	0.67
O	7	55.5	58.4	2.30	17.2	0.68
P	7½	56.5	59.5	2.35	17.6	0.69
Q	8	58	60.9	2.40	18.0	0.71
R	8½	59	62.3	2.45	18.4	0.72
S	9	60	63.4	2.50	18.8	0.74
T	9½	61	64.8	2.55	19.2	0.76
U	10	62.5	65.9	2.60	19.6	0.77
V	10½	64	67.4	2.65	20.0	0.79
W	11	65	68.6	2.70	20.4	0.80
X	11½	66	69.9	2.75	20.8	0.82
Y	12	68	71.2	2.80	21.2	0.83
Z	12½	69	72.4	2.85	21.6	0.85

Using ring blank measurements

Always add 1.5 times the thickness of the metal you are using to the length of the ring blank required for a particular size, to ensure accurate results. When measuring a finger, use a measuring gauge that is a similar width to the ring you are making – a wide band ring will need to be a larger size to fit over the knuckle than a thin band.

Temperatures

°F	°C	°F	°C
32	0	1100	593
100	38	1200	649
150	66	1300	704
200	93	1400	760
250	121	1500	816
300	149	1600	871
350	177	1700	927
400	204	1800	982
450	232	1900	1038
500	260	2000	1093
550	288	2250	1232
600	216	2500	1371
650	343	2750	1510
700	371	3000	1649
800	427	3250	1788
900	482	3500	1927
1000	538	4000	2204

Wire gauge (Brown & Sharpe)

B&S GAUGE	INCHES		MILLIMETRES
	Thou.	Fractions	
–	0.787	51/64	20.0
–	0.591	19/32	15.0
1	0.394	13/32	10.0
4	0.204	13/64	5.2
6	0.162	5/32	4.1
8	0.129	⅛	3.2
10	0.102	3/32	2.6
12	0.080	5/64	2.1
14	0.064	1/16	1.6
16	0.050	–	1.3
18	0.040	3/64	1.0
20	0.032	1/32	0.8
22	0.025	–	0.6
24	0.020	–	0.5
26	0.016	1/64	0.4
28	0.013	–	0.3
30	0.010	–	0.25

Some useful measurements

STANDARD SIZES OF	mm	inches
Diameter of earring posts and wires	0.8–0.9	0.031–0.035
Necklace lengths	400	16
	450	18
	500	20
Bracelet lengths	175	7
	190	7.5
	200	8.5
Bangle diameters	60	2.4
	65	2.6
	70	2.8

Temperature conversion formula

- To convert Celsius to Fahrenheit: Multply by 9, divide by 5, add 32
- To convert Fahrenheit to Celsius: Subtract 32, multiply by 5, divide by 9

Geometry formulas

- To find the circumference of a circle from the diameter: Circumference = 3.14 x diameter
- To find the area of a circle: Area = 3.14 x radius^2
- To find the diameter of a circle used to make a dome: Outside diameter of sphere minus thickness of metal x 1.43
  e.g., 18mm outside diameter, 0.6 thickness:
  18 − 0.6 = 17.4 ; 17.4 x 1.43 = 25mm
  If less accuracy is required, add the diameter of the dome to its height to find the approximate diameter of circle needed.

Converting weight of wax to cast metal

When using a wax model for casting, weigh the wax on accurate scales and use the following multipliers to calculate the approximate weight of the final piece:

- Sterling silver: x 10.5
- 9-carat yellow gold: x 11.2
- 18-carat yellow gold: x 15.5
- Palladium: x 12
- Platinum: x 22

Health and safety

In the workplace and in educational institutions, health and safety measures are strictly enforced – for good reason! If working in a home workshop, you should be just as rigorous. Before starting any process, think about how it can be conducted safely. Is there adequate ventilation? What personal protection should be worn? Is there a fire extinguisher on hand? Is there a well-stocked first-aid kit nearby?

The internet is a valuable resource – safety data sheets are available online for practically every chemical and material, and these include a section on what to do if an accident or spillage occurs.

Common sense is a valuable asset. Always tie hair up when working in the workshop; wear work shoes rather than sandals; have adequate protective equipment such as gloves, aprons, masks and respirators on hand. Don't eat or drink in the workshop.

SAFETY NOTES FOR WORKING WITH ACIDS

Acids must be treated with respect. They will quickly burn skin, can seriously damage eyes and destroy clothes.

Acids can produce dangerous fumes and should only be used in a well-ventilated area – ideally in a fume cabinet.

Wear suitable gloves and goggles when handling acids. Latex gloves are NOT recommended for working with nitric acid because they offer little or no protection due to easy chemical penetration.

It is very important that acids should be added to water, not water to acid, as the latter can cause a violent reaction.

Should nitric acid come into contact with skin, wash it off right away with plenty of water. It will leave a yellow stain that can only be removed by wear or scrubbing. If it goes in the eyes, flush them with copious amounts of water and seek medical attention if irritation continues.

Store acids in clearly marked, sealed bottles. Contact with easily oxidisible substances (including many organic substances such as acetone, acetonitrile, various alcohols, dichloromethane and many others) may result in fires or explosions, so store them separately.

It is worth acquiring safety data sheets for any chemicals you might use in the jewellery studio.

Glossary

Acetone	A flammable liquid solvent, used for dissolving resin, stop-out varnish or setter's wax and permanent marker.
Alloy	A mixture of metals.
Annealing	The process of heating and cooling metal to render it malleable.
Anticlastic raising	The process of forging metal on a specialised stake so that its axes are stretched in opposite directions.
Assaying	The process of analysing an alloy to determine the proportion of precious metal present in it. Having analysed a piece of alloyed jewellery, an official Assay Office can give it an appropriate hallmark.
Base metal	Non-precious metal (or an alloy of), such as copper, aluminium, iron, nickel and zinc.
Bezel	A thin collar of metal used to hold a stone in a setting.
Blank	A shape cut or stamped from sheet metal.
	A plain, unadorned ring or bangle.
Borax	A mineral salt that mixes easily with water to create a flux that is essential for soldering jewellery.
Burnish	To polish by rubbing, usually with a polished steel tool.
Carat	A unit of weight for measuring gemstones (0.2 gram).
	A measure of the purity of gold – pure gold is 24 carat. 18-carat gold is an alloy that contains 18 parts of pure gold in 24 parts of the alloy.
Chasing	The process of punching a relief design in metal from the front.
Chenier	Thin metal tube, often used for making hinges in jewellery. It can also form other parts, such as a stone setting.
Collet	A conical metal band that surrounds and supports a stone.
Culet	The small facet on the base of some brilliant-cut stones.
Doming	The process of curving sheet metal into spherical forms, most commonly used to create hollow beads.
Draw plate	A hardened steel plate with a series of holes in various sizes. Wire is drawn through the plate to reduce its thickness, or to change its shape. Draw plates are commonly available with round, square or rectangular holes.
Etching	The controlled corrosion of a surface with acid. In jewellery, the process is used to form surface decoration on metal. Some parts of the surface are protected by an acid-resisting substance, while others are eaten away by the acid.
Facet	A flat surface ground on a cut gemstone.
Ferrous	Containing iron.
Findings	Mass-produced jewellery components, such as catches, joints and clips, that are commonly used even on handmade jewellery. When such components are made by hand, they are sometimes called fittings.
Firestain/firescale	The grey coating that forms on silver when it is heated. The coating consists of copper oxide and is formed by the copper in the impure silver combining with oxygen in the air.
Flux	A substance used in soldering to ensure that the solder flows. Flux is applied to the parts to be soldered and prevents air from reaching them. As a result no oxides are formed, so the solder is able to flow and join the metal. Borax is the flux commonly used by jewellers.
Forging	The process of hammering metal to change its shape.
Former	A steel shape for supporting metal while it is being hammered. Formers are also known as mandrels.
Fume cupboard	A glass-fronted cupboard that has an extraction or air-filtration system inside, in which chemical processes such as etching are done.
Gauge	A standard unit of measurement of the thickness of sheet or the diameter of wire.

Girdle	The widest circumference of a gemstone. The girdle forms the boundary between the crown (top) and the pavillion (base).
Hallmark	A series of impressions made in an item of gold, silver or platinum. The hallmark is an official guarantee of the fineness of the metal.
Liver of sulphur	Potassium sulphide that can be dissolved in warm water to create a patina on silver and copper.
Malleability	The property, usually of a metal, of being easily hammered, rolled or pressed to shape without fracturing.
Mandrel	A former that can be used to provide a surface against which softer metal can be shaped.
Mordants	The general term for acids or chemicals that can etch metal.
Outwork	Processes or special professional services that are performed by someone else, for example plating or engraving.
Pallions	Small pieces of solder, taken from the French word for flake.
Patina	A surface finish that develops on metal or other material as a result of exposure to chemicals or handling.
Pickle	A solution used during construction to clean flux and oxides from metal after heating, such as after soldering. Pickle is also used to clean finished jewellery. Diluted sulphuric acid is often used as pickle.
Piercing saw	A saw with a blade narrow enough to be threaded through a drilled hole so that a pattern can be cut out from sheet metal or other material.
Planishing	The process of hammering metal with a polished hammer to obtain an even surface.
Repoussage	A relief design punched into thin metal from the back. The metal is often supported in a bowl of pitch.

Rouge	A polishing compound that is finely abrasive and used in the final stage of polishing.
Resists	A varnish or wax that will resist the corrosive effects of acids and can be used on metal to protect selected areas.
Reticulation	A process that uses the chemical structure of an alloy and heat to create a ridged, textured surface.
Shank	The part of a ring through which the finger passes.
Soldering	The process of joining metal using an alloy called solder. The solder is designed to melt at a temperature lower than the metal it is intended to join. The work and the solder are heated until the solder melts. On cooling, it solidifies to form a firm joint. The terms easy, medium and hard solder describe solders with progressively higher melting points. Thus, some joints can be made at a relatively low temperature without melting earlier joints made with a higher melting-point solder.
Sprue	The unwanted piece of metal attached to a casting and formed by the access channel in the mould.
Swaging	The process of making metal U-shaped by hammering it into a U-shaped groove on a metal block.
Tang	The end of a file, graver or tool that is fitted into a wooden handle.
Tempering	The process of beating metal after hardening to reduce its brittleness.
Triblet	A tapered steel rod on which rings are shaped (also known as a ring mandrel).
Upsetting	A forging technique used to spread the end of a piece of rod.
Vulcaniser	A press used for compressing hot rubber to form moulds for casting.
Work-hardening	The hardening of a metal caused by hammering or bending, which often makes the metal too hard to work with until it has been softened by annealing.

Index